"Are you terrified abou[t] ... ; book is a great primer, helping you av[oid] ... [too pus]hy or too passive, while training you in ... [confid]ent ways to explain the reasons for the hope you have."

James Choung, author of *True Story,* national director of evangelism, InterVarsity Christian Fellowship/USA

"I've read many books on evangelism, and there are very, very few that breathe the rarified air of being beneficial for our generation. This is one. In *Beyond Awkward*, Beau does a great job of covering important truths, points and questions in sharing the goodness of Jesus with others, and getting past the feeling of awkwardness in our conversations. We need more books like this one."

Matt Brown, evangelist and founder of Think Eternity

"For those who have already made the paradigm shift of what it means to be sent people, living incarnationally and demonstrating the love of Jesus, *Beyond Awkward* is a great next step in practically proclaiming the gospel to those we come in contact with on a daily basis. Evangelism tends to have a scary connotation, making us uneasy or anxious because of what others may think. But Beau Crosetto helps us understand the importance of sharing our faith because of the one who has captured our hearts—Jesus. Why would we not want to share him and what he came to bring with others? Great, practical mustread. You will be glad you did!"

Laura Hairston, executive director, Forge America

"Long before meeting Beau Crosetto, I heard how God was using him to lead an evangelistic movement within InterVarsity. Beau is the real deal—a gifted evangelist with a passion to see lives eternally changed. The biblical role of the evangelist has little to do with spotlights and stadiums and everything to do with equipping God's people to boldly share Jesus. In *Beyond Awkward*, this is precisely what Beau is doing—equipping the saints. This book hits the trifecta: it's simple, biblical and practical. Read this book and join God's movement toward the supernatural reset our world needs today."

Nick Hall, founder and CEO, PULSE Movement

"Beau Crosetto lives what he teaches, and out of his life comes this powerful and inspiring book. He has helped thousands of people on campuses and in churches to get beyond their fears and awkwardness and into the zone of seeing God work to influence people toward Christ. You will love it!"

Rick Richardson, author of *Reimagining Evangelism*; director of the evangelism, leadership and church planting program, Wheaton College Graduate School

"The call to 'embrace awkwardness' may sound strange, but it could be just what many Christians need to hear. In this enjoyable, challenging and universally applicable book, Beau Crosetto empowers believers to step beyond their fears, learn to hear God's voice and enter the amazing journey of relational evangelism. As you move beyond awkward into evangelism action, your faith and joy will rise. Let's live out this book!"

John Teter, senior pastor, Fountain of Life Covenant Church

"With our hearts pumping and palms sweaty, Beau reminds us that on the other side of scared and awkward, evangelism is power and salvation through Jesus. With compelling stories from his own life, scriptural examples and practical tools for every Christian to use, *Beyond Awkward* is a primer on taking steps to trust the Holy Spirit to experience the joy of witness. I'm grateful that Beau has provided us with an inviting place to realize we aren't alone in the awkwardness but that Jesus is faithful to always meet us there and give courage to take risks for his glory."

Jessica Fick, regional evangelism coordinator, InterVarsity Christian Fellowship

"Whether taking the next step in a conversation with a skeptic or preaching to a crowd of a thousand, Beau continues to fire me up to share the good news. He is one of the most influential and gifted evangelists I have ever met. For anyone seeking to grow your faith and share Jesus with others, one interaction with Beau will inspire you. And this book is a solid interaction. Dive in . . . and reach out."

Matthew Nault, City Church of San Francisco

"Beau Crosetto has truly crafted a Holy Spirit–driven, inspirational, biblically based resource that should be put in the hands of every Christian student in the university. *Beyond Awkward* challenges us to take risks, alleviates excuses for not sharing Jesus and is replete with pragmatic examples and advice on sharing your faith in Jesus. Beau's understanding and articulation of the partnership of the Holy Spirit with us in evangelism is fresh and encouraging. This is one of the most significant books on evangelism I have read."

E. Scott Martin, national director, Chi Alpha Campus Ministries, USA

BEYOND AWKWARD

When Talking About Jesus
Is Outside Your Comfort Zone

BEAU CROSETTO

FOREWORD BY DAVE FERGUSON

IVP Books

An imprint of InterVarsity Press
Downers Grove, Illinois

InterVarsity Press
P.O. Box 1400, Downers Grove, IL 60515-1426
World Wide Web: www.ivpress.com
Email: email@ivpress.com

InterVarsity Press˚ is the book-publishing division of InterVarsity Christian Fellowship/USA˚, a movement of students and faculty active on campus at hundreds of universities, colleges and schools of nursing in the United States of America, and a member movement of the International Fellowship of Evangelical Students. For information about local and regional activities, visit www.intervarsity.org.

All Scripture quotations, unless otherwise indicated, are taken from THE HOLY BIBLE, NEW INTERNATIONAL VERSION˚, NIV˚ Copyright © 1973, 1978, 1984, 2011 by Biblica, Inc.˚ Used by permission. All rights reserved worldwide.

While all stories in this book are true, some names and identifying information in this book have been changed to protect the privacy of the individuals involved.

Cover design: Cindy Kiple
Interior design: Beth McGill
Images: © 3dbobber/iStockphoto

ISBN 978-0-8308-3688-8 (print)
ISBN 978-0-8308-9705-6 (digital)

Printed in the United States of America ♾

Library of Congress Cataloging-in-Publication Data

Crosetto, Beau, 1982-
  Beyond awkward : when talking about Jesus is outside your comfort zone / Beau Crosetto ; foreword by Dave Ferguson.
      pages cm
  Includes bibliographical references.
  ISBN 978-0-8308-3688-8 (pbk. : alk. paper)
  1. Witness bearing (Christianity) I. Title.
  BV4520.C76 2014
  248.5--dc23

                                                            2014022824

P 20 19 18 17 16 15 14 13 12 11 10 9 8 7 6 5 4 3 2 1

Y 31 30 29 28 27 26 25 24 23 22 21 20 19 18 17 16 15 14

I dedicate this book to Noah and Sophia, my first two children.

May you grow up to be bold and loving witnesses for Christ.

I hope you have the opportunity to see many people

experience Jesus through your life and testimony.

Contents

Foreword

awk·ward: clumsy, inept, unskillful.

I can't think of a better word to describe many of my early evangelistic efforts than the word *awkward*.

Awkward Zealot

I was a freshman in college when Jesus became real to me. I was so blown away by God's grace and its power to change my past, present and future that I couldn't imagine keeping it to myself any more than I could imagine keeping the cure to cancer to myself. I had to get the good news out there so it could help the people who needed it!

With that unbridled motivation—and having recently been through an evangelism training program—I canvassed the University of Missouri campus. I stopped complete strangers on the sidewalk by asking them, "Have you come to the place in your spiritual life where you know for certain that if you were to die today, you would go to heaven?" After they stammered for an answer, I would counter with, "Suppose that you were to die today and stand before God and he were to ask you, 'Why should I let you in to my heaven?' What would you say?" I ambushed hundreds of people with those two questions in my bungling enthusiasm. Unfortunately, each conversation left me with the feeling that I was actually turning more people away from God than toward God. I was an awkward zealot.

I was on the way back to Missouri from Oklahoma City on a road trip with my college roommate when we slowed the car to pick up a hitchhiker. Relieved to get a ride, he jumped in the back seat and introduced himself: "Hi, I'm Bill." My first thought was, "I have a captive audience!"

Within minutes I had turned our conversation toward spiritual things. I tried the questions again, "Bill, have you come to the place in your spiritual life where you know for certain that if you were to die today, you would go to heaven?"

Bill admitted he didn't know that for sure. So I pounced on him with the second question: "Suppose that you were to die today and stand before God and he were to ask you, 'Why should I let you in to my heaven?' What would you say?"

Bill thought and said, "'Cause I've been a pretty good guy."

He had fallen into my evangelistic trap, and by the time we crossed over the state line and headed back to school, Bill had agreed to follow Jesus and be baptized. I was so excited that I told my roommate who was driving to take a detour to a local church where we baptized Bill before we even got back to our college dorm. I was on an evangelistic high!

However, the buzz only lasted till the next day when our wayfarer friend took twenty dollars out of my wallet and stole my roommate's car. We never saw him again.

Bill didn't believe. Bill didn't say "yes" to Jesus. He had duped this awkward zealot.

Awkward Silence

I think that might have been the turning point. My enthusiasm for Jesus and gratitude for God's grace didn't waver, but my evangelistic efforts went into a steep decline.

It was years later that I found myself leading a large church with a vibrant evangelistic mission of "helping people find their way back to God," but personally keeping silent about Jesus unless someone asked me. At one point I came to the realization that I had lived on my street for seven years and never mentioned anything about Jesus to anyone. I didn't invite anyone to church. I didn't have any spiritual conversations.

I had unconsciously made a choice that I wasn't going to risk being an awkward zealot. Instead I lived in an awkward silence. And my awkward silence yielded the same results as my years as an awkward zealot: I was pointing almost no one to God.

Beyond Awkward

Perhaps you find yourself feeling awkward in your attempts to share Jesus. Maybe, like me, you have been awkwardly zealous and have seen people turn away from Jesus and spiritual things. Or maybe you can relate to the awkward silence because you know what it is like to live or work near people who have never heard you say one word about Jesus. If either of those are you, then you have picked up the right book!

Beau Crosetto is the perfect person to author *Beyond Awkward*. Beau is a passionate and gifted evangelist who loves introducing people to Jesus. What Beau loves even more is equipping people like us who often find ourselves either overzealous or too quiet in how to share our faith. *Beyond Awkward* is a great handbook, by a terrific evangelist, that equips the rest of us to evangelize more effectively.

Beau challenges us to enter in to the awkwardness of spiritual encounters. He rightly suggests that all of us need to be prepared for those God moments, and he asks the poignant question: "Who is just waiting for you to tell them about Jesus?" In the pages to come you will discover your part and the Spirit of God's part in every spiritual encounter.

Once you finish the pages of *Beyond Awkward*, you may never again find yourself acting as an awkward zealot or quietly living in an awkward silence. Through inspiring stories, practical tools and a strong dose of motivation you will be equipped and ready when you meet the person who is just waiting for you to share Jesus with them.

Dave Ferguson
Lead pastor, Community Christian Church
Spiritual entrepreneur, NewThing

Introduction

I REMEMBER WHEN my kids were born how happy I was to share with the world the good news. Whether it was a text, a tweet or a Facebook photo, I was proud to be a dad and wanted people to know it.

You and I have no problem telling people every day about incredible things that are affecting our lives. A new child is born, an achievement is made, a great movie was seen, the best meal was eaten. We regularly tell our friends, "You have to go see that movie! Please!"

We are evangelists for many great things. Just not Jesus.

Jesus is awkward for most of us. Let's be honest. He is the topic most of us want to avoid in public. He's like that uncle who is really funny *inside* the family circle, but if you're honest, you would rather not take him anywhere.

Jesus is private. Jesus is not to be pushed. He should stay inside his little book.

But deep down you also know he is great news. He is changing your life, he is giving you purpose, and he has saved your soul. You know he is good news for you, so why isn't he good news for your friends or family? Why are we uncomfortable sharing him with others, but

We are evangelists for many great things. Just not Jesus.

we'll recommend a good restaurant? Why are we not free to speak of Jesus like we are with so many other topics?

Why is Jesus private while nothing else great in our lives is? I'll give you three reasons.

First, your image of people who share Jesus isn't good. The pictures you have of evangelists are most likely TV preachers asking for money, angry people picketing with offensive signs or salesmen pushing a slick gospel. Who wants to be like that?

Second, you feel like we share Jesus under our own power. You believe you have to muster up the strength, get a better script and deliver a killer argument. Who wants all that pressure?

Third, you simply don't know how to do it. Most people have never been shown how to turn an everyday conversation into a respectful one about Jesus. Most people have never been taught how to share the good news in a helpful way. Who wants to feel like an idiot?

In this book I hope to give you (1) a better image of an evangelist, (2) a better understanding of God's leading in your life, and (3) very practical tools for sharing the good news of Jesus in relational and respectful ways.

I hope to move you not only beyond the awkward feelings but through them so you can break through to the people who touch your life every day.

This Works

I have taught seminar after seminar on this content to college students and churchgoers. It seems to work well with any age group. I have received excellent feedback about what has been helpful and inspiring, as well as what can be better and more practical. It's all in this book. I am excited about this book because the content shared is actually working on campus, in the workplace and in families across the world.

As you read this book, be encouraged and expect that God will give you some tested principles for sharing your faith in today's culture.

Release the APE

One of the main reasons I am passionate about this book is that I see it as my calling to raise up and release apostolic, prophetic and evangelistic people. In fact, I started a blog (www.releasetheape .com) dedicated to doing this.

I started this blog because historically we have relied too much on the *shepherd* and *teacher* roles in the church. To be clear, I love teachers and shepherds, and we desperately need them in the church. But we cannot advance the mission of Jesus very well by activating only 40 percent of the callings given by Christ as Ephesians 4 tells us. In almost every church the leaders are called teachers or pastors/shepherds. Why? Especially when *shepherd* is mentioned a few times in the New Testament and *pastor* not at all. These titles are deficient by themselves.

In Ephesians 4 Jesus is fully reflected on earth when the body of Christ carries out five functions: apostle, prophet, evangelist, shepherd and teacher. But we are empowering only two of them today. If we are serious about the Great Commission, we must be serious about all five. They *all* need to be released. First, because we can't reflect Jesus fully without them. Second, with regard to mission, the apostle, prophet and evangelist roles are the most catalytic and do the most to advance it.

- The apostle is an entrepreneur: starting new things as the chief architect of mission.
- The prophet oversees quality control: making sure values stick and that the mission is true.
- The evangelist manages public relations: in touch with the public and pushing forward the brand.
- The shepherd takes care of human relations: making sure everyone is cared for and is growing well.
- The teacher is a trainer: ensuring that all know how to do their job and understand what the company is about.

Obviously a great organization needs all these roles; so does the church. An overreliance on the shepherd and teacher leads to great Bible teaching and counseling, but not much mission advancement or connecting new people to Christ. It's time we activate all five vocations so all people are reached and cared for!

As we zero in on evangelism in this book, it is important to understand that sharing our faith feels awkward because this calling has not been empowered well. To many of us evangelism feels just as awkward and overwhelming as would starting a new church or giving a prophetic word. We haven't done a great job inspiring people toward these callings, providing language to talk about them or shaping a genuine path to move forward effectively in evangelism.

Embracing Awkward—Learning from Philip

The first part of *Beyond Awkward* will prepare you for the spiritual conversations awaiting you. Two crucial things must happen. You have to embrace awkwardness, which is the gateway to many breakthroughs with people around you. Second, you have to realize that people are actually waiting for you. People all around you are desperate for answers and guidance, and if you grab hold of that reality, you will be prepared to step into the God moments waiting to happen.

Most of the time when we talk about sharing the faith, we feel that it is all up to us. However, the Holy Spirit is a major player in all conversations and conversions. He is orchestrating encounters with seekers, and our job is to hear his voice and follow.

Philip is a great example of a bold witness who was discerning and relational. After we talk about preparing for God moments, we will dive into the story of Philip and extract principles from his encounter with the Ethiopian eunuch in Acts 8. How was he able to follow the Spirit when the outcome was so unclear? We will see that Philip was obedient to the Spirit, used discernment in the encounter with the Ethiopian and was skilled in talking about Jesus.

In the last chapter I also drill down into practical tools to help Christians see how to turn casual conversations into eternal encounters. The six chapters in this section are devoted to walking through the practical aspects of turning casual conversations into Jesus conversations.

Inspiring Stories

I hope to inspire you with faith that these types of evangelistic encounters can happen in your everyday life. Nearly every chapter begins with an inspiring story, and scattered throughout the book are testimonies of everyday people who are actively sharing their faith. You'll hear from a businessperson, a mother and a young professional. You'll also hear a former NFL quarterback, an ESPN broadcaster and an emergency-room doctor sharing their faith in their respective contexts.

Their stories inspire me, and I know they will do the same for you. My hope is that anyone reading this book will be able to put it down and say, "I have no excuse. I can talk about Jesus too."

Key Steps and Reflection Questions

Every chapter suggests a key step or two for you or your small group to take that week. You will also find questions to help you become a better witness and live in tune with the Spirit. So much of sharing our faith is taking risks and reflecting well. Discernment comes from being more perceptive about what is happening in and around us. Each chapter ends in a practical way so you can take another step forward.

My hope is that the stories, reflections and next steps will better activate evangelism in the church and help us to have better language and methods to carry forward the Great Commission.

1

Someone Is Waiting for You

I WAS ONCE ON A FLIGHT seated next to a man who leads Himalayan tours for a living. He talked for an hour about living year round in the mountains and guiding tour groups. The tourists come and go, but he stays. He lives alone, has no family and no real community. He told me repeatedly that he doesn't talk to people much and that he and I were having one of the longest conversations he had had in years. I felt the spiritual opportunity rising.

As the flight continued, he shared many spiritual thoughts and asked great questions. I had legitimate responses about why I think Jesus is the answer to his questions. God was prompting me by his Spirit to provide the man with answers. But I never did. I was too nervous. I felt awkward. I was more concerned about what others would think of me than I was about this guy's eternal destiny. I was worried what the people behind us and in front of us would think if I started talking about Jesus. I flashed forward to the baggage claim where people might stare me down as if to say, "So *you* are that annoying Jesus freak talking on the plane."

I froze. I never gave him a single answer. Instead, I said stuff like, "Great questions, man. I'm sure that someday you'll find the answers you are looking for."

Missing the Moment

To this day, I kick myself for chickening out. I hate that moment because I know too much now. I know that people are waiting for a witness, and God is waiting to pour his love onto them through that witness. That flight could have been a conversion moment. The man was definitely searching for spiritual answers and could very well have been curious, ready to hear the gospel and accept it on the spot. But instead of following the Spirit's promptings, I let the opportunity drop, hit the floor and roll down the aisle.

God does give grace, of course, when we make mistakes and miss the moments he has prepared. This book was written so that we miss as few of those moments as possible.

Imagine what this guy is potentially missing because I didn't have the courage to respond to an open moment. He could be experiencing the profound love of Jesus that brings security and peace even when he is alone. He could have the transforming power of God's Spirit. Who knows the ways this guy needs sanctification and change? When the Spirit of God indwells us after we start a relationship with Jesus, he is faithful to complete the good work in our life.

> In all my prayers for all of you, I always pray with joy because of your partnership in the gospel from the first day until now, being confident of this, that he who began a good work in you will carry it on to completion until the day of Christ Jesus. (Philippians 1:4-6)

I hate that this guy didn't have an opportunity to know Jesus that day on the plane. Though I had great answers, I froze. I was too worried and didn't have my mind right. He missed out on learning about the best news in the world—a good, loving, forgiving and transforming God will never leave us—because of my fear.

If you have had your fair share of moments like mine, times when you knew you needed to speak but kept quiet, or when you knew you needed to step forward but you froze, please keep reading. I hope to equip you to be bold when the Lord calls you to action. People eager to hear the good news about Jesus are waiting for you.

My Dad Was Waiting

So much happened during my first month of college: I made new friends, partied hard, enjoyed meeting the guys on my golf team and—lo and behold—became a Christian.

People eager to hear the good news about Jesus are waiting for you.

When I came into relationship with Jesus, the passion and urgency to share my faith was activated in me. I was floored by the fact that we could know God and have a relationship with him. He could save us from our sins, would judge us no more and set us free from unhealthy patterns. I couldn't wait to share what I'd found, but I had no clue what to say; I didn't know any Bible verses and barely knew my own testimony. I did know, however, that everyone needed a relationship with the all-knowing God incarnated in Jesus Christ.

The second weekend of October was fall break, so I went home for the weekend to see my family.

My first night home I was sitting in the kitchen with my dad, telling him about everything that had happened during the first month of school. Then something strange happened. As I was leaning against the island in the kitchen and Dad was sitting in his usual chair watching the ball game, he paused the game and asked me about my relationship with God and wanted to know more.

I was surprised and caught off-guard. Most people find it difficult to talk about this type of stuff with their parents. *How do I explain to my parents about my newfound faith in God? Shouldn't they be explaining religion to me?* But I was also excited. I mean, of course I wanted to tell Dad about Jesus and help him know the joy that I had found.

As I began to explain how I had decided to follow Jesus, Dad interrupted me and said, "Son, if you are going to be in heaven, I want to be in heaven too."

As you can imagine, it was an emotional moment. As I was holding back tears, we hugged, and then I prayed with him to receive Jesus.

I had no idea Dad was waiting for a moment like that, but he was. I couldn't believe he was so open to God and that it could be that easy to see someone come to faith, especially my father. What I thought might be the hardest case was actually one of the easiest I have had. God totally surprised me that night, and going forward it changed the way I thought about sharing Jesus with people.

I know it is not usually that easy, but God used that experience to do something powerful in me at the start of our relationship: he showed me that it is possible to lead others to faith, and that many people are open. More than that, God revealed that people are waiting for a witness.

This theme has continued throughout my Christian life. Even though countless other encounters since have not been nearly as easy as my conversation with Dad, God has solidified in me the belief that he can use each of us to lead people to Christ. He also revealed to me that people who don't attend church are also ready to come to faith, but they need someone to meet them right where they are. Just like I talked to my dad *in our kitchen*, God can and will bring people to faith anywhere. Getting them to church may not be possible, for a variety of reasons, but unwillingness to visit a church does not mean that they are not open to spiritual conversation and giving their life to Jesus.

Church is often the last place that someone who is checking out Jesus wants to go.

Church is often the last place that someone who is checking out Jesus wants to go. It can be a place full of bad memories, it can signal power differentials that make them uncomfortable, or it can even get in the way of an authentic conversation as they resort to past scripts playing in their head. Church sometimes can be the hardest place for a seeking person to hear fresh expressions of the gospel. This is why we need to keep thinking creatively and missionally about how to incarnate the gospel by dwelling among the people around us. Instead of resorting to taking people to church, how can we create safe discussions in our neighborhoods, at work, on campus or even in a bar? Some people will need this first step before going to church.

One Key Question: Who Is Waiting for You?

Imagine what your life would be like if you were being used by God to have effective spiritual conversations with people. Imagine people greeting you in heaven by saying, "Thank you for introducing me to Jesus." This can be more than a dream. God is calling you to reach specific people he wants to be in relationship with. People you are perfectly designed or positioned to reach—even though you don't know the Bible inside and out, or your testimony isn't smooth, or whatever else you feel excludes you from being used by God in this way.

God wants you to point others to Jesus in everyday places. He may be positioning you to reach people on your street, in your workplace, on your teams, at your college or among your circle of friends. You may be thinking of people in these places who don't seem to be open now, but some of them are indeed waiting for a witness. They are waiting for you to show up, to open your mouth and to explain to them who Jesus is and what he can do for them.

I want to be the kind of person God uses regularly, and you want to be that kind of person too. You can, but there is something you have to get over first: feeling awkward. The fear of what people will think of you for sharing your faith is real and limiting. It can grab you by the throat and cause you not to speak, not to be bold or even not to take the first step toward others.

The best way to move past the uncomfortable feelings that arise in sharing your faith is to understand why sharing your faith is worth it in the first place. We are going to do this in the next chapter. When you understand why it is worth the tension and what really is at stake, maybe you can take that next step of boldness and partner with God in talking with a friend about Jesus.

Reflection Questions

1. Describe a time when you helped a person in need. Why did you do it, and how did that feel?

2. Can you think of a time when you missed a moment? Describe what thoughts or feelings blocked you.

3. Imagine yourself discovering an open person at work, in your class or in your neighborhood. Do you believe that it is worth feeling awkward in order to help them understand God better? Why?

4. Pray for a moment about this week. Ask God who you should pray for.

A WITNESS AT WORK
Down the Medical Road

Evelyn Lo, ER doctor

"I'm always on the lookout for God encounters with my patients." As a physician, Evelyn Lo has had to learn to navigate the fine line between the personal and professional. She finds it most effective to share her faith with her patients by engaging in conversation that provokes questions. When her patients start asking her questions, Evelyn is free to share her faith.

One time a man came to her ER wanting detox. He launched into a story about how he had been held at gunpoint and robbed of $16,000. He escaped without harm and wandered the streets aimlessly until a man asked him how he was doing. Of course he replied "not good," and the man then pointed him into a Narcotics Anonymous meeting in the church right behind them. The man went to the NA meeting and the leader sent him to the ER for detox.

Enter Evelyn.

Evelyn says that she is always looking for an on ramp as she listens to patients' stories, and this time God led her to ask, "Why do you think God saved your life?" Immediately he began to cry and unpacked more of his story for Evelyn. At that moment she was able to pray with him and share the gospel. That night he accepted Christ into his life.

"God is always at work around you," Evelyn learned from the book *Experiencing God* by Henry Blackaby. "He invites us to work with him."

2

Is It Worth It?

A**LTHOUGH** I **HAD DABBLED** in Christian activities for a few years right before college, I was not yet a Christian when I arrived at the University of San Diego.

I was excited to have a golf scholarship and play the beautiful courses around the city free. But golf courses weren't the only beautiful thing I was looking for. The campus was 70 percent female, so I knew my chances were good. I was the typical freshman male: I had girls and golf, but not much God, on my mind.

My first day on campus was two weeks before school started. I was in the weight room (getting ready for golf and the girls), when a guy wearing a Young Life shirt caught my attention and sparked my curiosity. I had been to Young Life, a high school ministry, before college and liked it, so I thought this guy might be a cool dude to meet since I didn't yet know anyone. I decided to spark a conversation with him.

"What's up, man? My name is Beau. So, you do Young Life?"

He responded in a friendly way, "Actually, I don't. This is my roommate's shirt, and I just coincidentally threw it on today because all of mine were dirty. I am actually part of InterVarsity on campus. Why? What's up?"

Coincidentally? If not for that shirt, I never would have talked to him.

Charlie, the shirt borrower, was the first person I met in college, and he helped me find the Lord. He was a junior and quickly got me connected to InterVarsity Christian Fellowship (a campus ministry) and in a small group. He met with me and talked with me about my questions. He connected me to other Christians, like the captain of the soccer team, who met with me every Tuesday night over sandwiches so I could grill him with my questions and doubts.

That one conversation in the weight room forever changed my life. It was all because God had intersected a seeker like me with a witness like Charlie. I was longing for good news, a bigger story and connection with God. I look back on those first days of college and thank God for Charlie's willingness to share with me his belief that Jesus was great news. In Charlie's mind, Jesus was worth sharing.

But I also think about what my life would have been like if Charlie hadn't shared Jesus with me. What if he had been embarrassed or timid about Jesus? What if he hadn't been persistent in calling me and inviting me to InterVarsity and church? What if he had just let the moment pass? I could have missed out on this great news!

People are waiting for you to help them know Jesus.

This book is called *Beyond Awkward* because, let's face it, sharing our faith can be and often is more than awkward—it's scary and terrifying. So the first question we need to ask ourselves before continuing is, *Is it worth it?* This message, this God-man, better be worth it. If he's not, we are all wasting our time sharing the message.

Jesus is worth it. He is great news, and that is why I share him freely. I share it even though it takes me into some sticky situations.

But it takes some digging to understand why there is tension and where it is coming from. Why do we love God so much but have such an aversion to talking about him in public? Do I believe Jesus is worth it? Why do I believe this? What is blocking me from being free in my ability to talk about him?

> **Jesus is worth it. He is great news.**

God is missional, and in the Bible—cover to cover—we find

ourselves encountering a sending God who regularly invites his people to take giant risks for his name so the kingdom of God can be extended.

People who step out and follow Jesus into witness understand that because God is sending them, the reward outweighs the risk. They know he leads to life. Even if it costs me some or all of my life, the God of the Bible brings others to life in Christ through people who risk.

People who step out for Jesus understand how incredibly good he is and that his plans, no matter how scary they may look, always lead to blessing someone—either the receiver or the witness. Even if God's call causes pain, persecution or discomfort, the part the witness plays in mission is worth it because God is releasing life through the witness's obedience.

People who shrink back from bold moments get stuck in their discomfort and choose to believe that their feelings are the end of the story. But people who step out for Jesus believe that the amount of tension they have to take on is less than the amount of joy someone else will receive from their obedience.

One of my favorite movies is *Braveheart*, and in that movie the main character, William Wallace, risks everything, including his own life, because he believes the freedom of his people is worth it. He knows what is at stake, but he believes the future joy that could ensue is worth more than his temporary life.

If you believe God is in the business of releasing incredible joy into people's lives, you will take on more awkwardness for the sake of seeing others encounter Jesus.

The following is a story of a few people who saw firsthand that stepping out for Jesus is worth it.

Water into Wine

Jesus did his first miracle in Cana by turning water into wine. In this story we see why he is such great news.

On the third day a wedding took place at Cana in Galilee.
Jesus' mother was there, and Jesus and his disciples had also
been invited to the wedding. When the wine was gone, Jesus'
mother said to him, "They have no more wine."

"Woman, why do you involve me?" Jesus replied. "My time has
not yet come."

His mother said to the servants, "Do whatever he tells you."
(John 2:1-5)

Weddings in Jesus' day were not your typical one-evening affair.
They lasted up to a week. Running out of wine in the middle of the
celebration would be not only embarrassing and rude, but also
shameful for the family. It was a crisis, to say the least. When these
people found out they'd run out of wine, they had no immediate
solution. Jesus' mother, aware of the great need, sprang into action
and alerted her son to do something.

Nearby stood six stone water jars, the kind used by the Jews for
ceremonial washing, each holding from twenty to thirty gallons.

Jesus said to the servants, "Fill the jars with water"; so they
filled them to the brim.

Then he told them, "Now draw some out and take it to the
master of the banquet." (vv. 6-8)

In response to Mary's request, Jesus turned close to 180 gallons
of water into wine. (For those of you in a fraternity, that would be
eleven kegs.) Not only was this an absurd amount of wine for a
wedding coming to a close, it was better than the wine served
earlier—it was "choice wine."

The master of the banquet tasted the water that had been turned
into wine. He did not realize where it had come from, though
the servants who had drawn the water knew. Then he called the
bridegroom aside and said, "Everyone brings out the choice

wine first and then the cheaper wine after the guests have had too much to drink; but you have saved the best till now." (vv. 9-10)

No one saves the best wine for late into a celebration. Even in today's party culture it's common to start with the good stuff early, while your guests can appreciate the taste. Once the party is well underway, the Franzia (a popular boxed wine) gets served. Jesus reversed the norm by giving the party not only much more wine than they needed but also the best.

Why did he do this? What was Jesus trying to tell us about himself and our Father in heaven by turning water into wine? "What Jesus did here in Cana of Galilee was the first of the signs through which he revealed his glory; and his disciples believed in him" (v. 11).

Something about this miracle was a sign pointing to the nature of God. We know *glory* is the fullness of God, and Jesus revealed that fullness in this miracle.

A Generous God

If turning 180 gallons of water into the best wine tells us anything about God, it certainly tells us he is generous. He is a God who lavishes us with more than enough at just the right time. Whether we think we are about to (or already have) hit bottom, or we aren't even aware we are close to the bottom (the master of the banquet didn't know the wine had run out), God will save us. Not only will he save us, he will do it with more than enough and with the best of what we need.

This raises more questions: What is God saving us from, and what is he saving us with? Why is Jesus using water and wine? Why is he using the metaphor of a nearly ruined party? And why did Jesus give such a strange answer when his mother declared there was no more wine? Jesus is playing with words to point to a bigger story. The wine running out is a metaphor for the reality of the world and what he will do to save it, namely, go to the cross. But his time had not yet come for that bigger mission. He was just starting his journey—it was only chapter two.

But Jesus had a little fun at the wedding to show us what he can do. In Scripture wine is a common metaphor for sustenance, blessing and wrath. Throughout the Old Testament wine was given by God to sustain the Israelites and was closely tied with their obedience (Deuteronomy 28–29). Furthermore, the prophets used the imagery of wine to reveal God's eschatological blessing as well as his wrath being poured out (Jeremiah 25:15; Joel 3:18; Amos 9:13).

So, beyond saving the party at Cana, Jesus is boldly declaring that he would save the world when his time came. The water-into-wine miracle foreshadows Jesus pouring out an overabundance of his blood for the forgiveness of sins and release from God's wrath. His forgiveness is not only overflowing but of the highest quality: free and everlasting.

Jesus extended the metaphor by using water from the ceremonial washing jars. This signaled that we could be cleansed through him. A relationship with God and connection to the Father would be through the blood of Jesus.

Jesus can and has come to save the day. He has an overabundance of forgiveness and love to pour out on the world, whether those in it know it or not. Jesus has been invited to the failing party, and he can and wants to turn it around.[1] God has made Jesus the Lord of the universe, and one day he will create new heavens and a new earth. He wants to bring as many people as possible with him into the eternal party.

Bold Servants Are Needed

> Jesus has been invited to the failing party, and he can and wants to turn it around.

A sneaky detail in this story lies with the servants. Consider two things: (1) the servants had to carry the water to the master of the banquet, and (2) they alone knew how the water turned to wine. The servants got a front-row seat to Jesus' first miracle.

Jesus asked the servants to carry water to the master of the banquet. What does this reveal about Jesus? And what does the servants' obedience tell us about them? If that water hadn't turned to wine, these servants might have been beaten or even fired. Think about how angry their master would have been. But something led the servants to believe in Jesus' power.

The servants are the linchpin. Yes, Jesus had the power to turn the party around, but if the servants didn't carry the water, the miracle wouldn't have happened. They risked their reputations on Jesus' word.

In his mission to reach the world Jesus will call on us to play specific roles that no one else can play, scary, nerve-racking roles with much on the line. But it's not just an invitation into something crazy, it's also an invitation to witness an incredible miracle. Bold servants are needed in our world—servants who will carry the gospel of Jesus in the same way the servants carried the water that turned into wine.

Like the servants, Jesus will ask us to do things that don't make sense and will cripple us if he doesn't come through. Many of us believe a safe Jesus will ask us to do things that only make sense and will make us happy. But the picture of Jesus in John 2 points to the contrary. Jesus asked these servants to risk it all and trust that he would come through. It was the only way the party was going to be saved.

Will You Risk It?

The lives of many people around you are falling apart. They have run out of wine in some area of their life. Maybe a family member has died, divorce is imminent, cancer has struck or they are stuck in an addictive sin. They need the abundantly good God to rescue them.

But even if their wine hasn't run out in an immediate or clear way, the biblical narrative is clear that all people have run out spiritually. All of us have fallen short of the glory of God, and all of us need Jesus (Romans 3:23-24). Jesus sees the ways people around you have run out, and he wants to act. And he wants us to bring them his new wine. All along, God's plan has been to use people, and there's no backup plan. Jesus uses people to reach people. You won't find a single person in the New Testament who came to faith in Jesus without hearing the gospel from another person.[2]

You get to be the servant who carries this good news to others. People need to know that Jesus has the best love and forgiveness this world can find. And he has more than enough to give. They need to be invited into his eternal kingdom.

> **You won't find a single person in the New Testament who came to faith in Jesus without hearing the gospel from another person.**

But the reality is this: If you don't believe that Jesus gives the highest quality and most abundant forgiveness, healing, love and grace to desperate and hurting people, then you won't risk your reputation and introduce them to Jesus. If you don't believe the invitation into Jesus' eternal kingdom is the best gift you could give, then you won't be willing to pay the price to share the good news with them.

The servants in John 2 moved forward because they had to—it was their job. You too need to move forward as Jesus calls, because it is your job as well to partner with him in mission and in saving "parties." But it is more than just our job as disciples, it is an opportunity to partner with and sit in the front row as God unleashes something wonderful. Don't you want to see this kind of action? The risk is worth the reward for the servants in John 2. You too will move forward and share your faith with your friends if you believe the reward—God's free gift of salvation—is worth the risk.

> **The gospel of Jesus has to be good news for us first in order for us to share it with others.**

We have to believe it, wrestle with it, experience it and know it. The gospel of Jesus has to be good news for us first in order for us to share it with others.

It's Worth It

I have walked hundreds of people through John 2, and it is by far my favorite story to share with seekers. It is pure joy for me. It's hard to contain my smile on days I know I'll be sharing John 2 with someone. On those days I know I will have the opportunity to share an abundantly good God who saves lives.

One person I had the opportunity to share with is Alan.

Alan's relationships had run out, and his party had crashed. He was in need of renewal and knew it. But he felt hopeless. I remember waking up excited that I was going to deliver the best news Alan had ever heard. What a privilege, I thought, that Alan wanted answers that I was able to deliver. I knew he was nervous, but I knew Jesus would deliver.

I was a little nervous too, of course, but I knew my job. I was the carrier of the message. Evangelism isn't forcing Jesus on people but carrying the message of Jesus forward and letting him turn it to wine. I didn't need to make anything happen, I just needed to be willing to share and to respond to Alan's question about how to find a meaningful life.

I walked Alan through John 2 and helped him see Jesus' extravagant bailout plan. Alan and I both laughed when I told him Jesus turned the dud of a party into an eleven-keg "rager." But Alan got serious when I told him that the reality of the wedding-party story is that Jesus can turn our empty, crashed out, hopeless lives into ones full of extravagant joy and meaning.

I knew Alan wanted this Jesus. I could see it in his eyes. He wanted hope. He wanted forgiveness. He loved the idea that Jesus had plenty of both.

So I told him, "Jesus is the one who gives great wine, man."

We laughed.

"Really, though, Jesus is the one who gives an abundance of forgiveness and joy," I said. "He has plenty of healing and love for you. He proved it on the cross. His blood shed for you and me, so that we could stay eternally full. Jesus has an overflowing vat of this stuff for us. All we have to do is turn to him and ask him to start filling us up. His forgiveness is free for us. All we have to do is ask Jesus for it, acknowledge we have run out and our sources don't work, and trust him that his does. Do you want that, Alan?"

Alan immediately responded yes.

I led him through a prayer of forgiveness, and he started a relationship with Jesus that day. We prayed for the love of Christ to fill his soul and to turn Alan's life of depravity into one that was a party instead. We thanked God that he is so good and went on our way. Now Alan is an active witness telling others about this extravagant love and joy that God has to offer.

No Better Feeling

There is no better feeling than leading someone into the abundant presence of Jesus. I mean that. Yes, it is scary at times, and it sometimes feels like being a servant carrying water to someone expecting wine. But the joy at the end is unmatched.

Seeing the beginning of someone's new life with Jesus is difficult to describe. Every time I help someone start a relationship with Jesus, I feel so full. It's like the

> **There is no better feeling than leading someone into the abundant presence of Jesus.**

clearest understanding of purpose fills my soul in that instant. What better use of time is there than to help someone who doesn't know God become connected to him and his love? What better risk is there than one that could have eternal benefits? I've come to crave these moments when friends encounter Jesus—when the sparkle of hope appears in their eyes. It's like watching water turn to wine.

I long for you to experience this too. It's worth it. It's worth the awkward tension; it's worth the haunting fears. It's worth the risk. I hope you are willing to engage and move past the awkwardness, because people have run out of life and need their parties restored! They are waiting for you to deliver the gospel message.

Key Step: Make a List

Make a list of five people you know who don't have Jesus in their lives. Imagine what their lives could be like if Jesus were to fill them with his abundant goodness. Pray for each of them by name this week.

Reflection Questions

1. Make a list of ways that Jesus is good news to you.

2. How do you feel about sharing Jesus with people who don't follow him?

3. What strikes you about Jesus in John 2?

4. What do you need in order to feel like sharing Jesus is worth the risks?

A WITNESS AT WORK
Down the Over Fifty Road

George Toles, former NBA announcer
and advertising agency owner

George Toles is one of my heroes in the faith. When I think about growing older—well into my seventies—and having a legacy, I think of George. When he turned fifty, God nudged him, suggesting it was time to start a Bible study for all the people he had met during his twenty-two years in Seattle. So he did.

"We began inviting media types, realtors, bankers, attorneys and brokers to three lunches a year at the Washington Athletic Club. To our amazement, about forty came to each lunch, several of whom trusted Christ for the first time."

Well-known believers told their life story at these lunches, and those in attendance were invited to accept Christ. After two years or so of hosting these outreach events, George's wife, Liz, pointed out that these seekers and new believers were mostly unchurched and had little Bible knowledge. So for the next couple of decades George took almost fourteen hundred businessmen on interactive hikes through the Bible, first in a downtown boardroom, and now in a restaurant. These sessions have spawned lots of one-on-one counseling, mentoring and hospital visits.

"Our twice-monthly, ninety-minute lunches are unconventional, nonthreatening but biblically blunt." George posts study notes covering every book in the Bible and many topical issues online at www.hisdeal.org. His mission is to offer "a safe gathering place for men who are curious about Jesus Christ and what he taught."

Ask George how he feels about this risky adventure he set out on decades ago, and he'll tell you, "It's the most challenging, rewarding experience we've ever had. Why did I wait until I turned fifty?"

3

Evangelism Is Awkward

I WAS WALKING FROM MY CAR to my apartment when I noticed two missionaries talking to the girl who lived downstairs. My wife and I had never talked to her, but we had often heard her and her friends partying late into the night below us. As I was about to walk up the stairs, I sensed God asking me to wait for the missionaries to finish, and then talk to them. So I waited.

When they were done talking to my neighbor, they walked toward me. I could tell they were excited to see me and have the chance to talk. I asked right away about what they had been saying to my neighbor. They told me that they had come to proclaim the end times—that Jesus had come again and was now in Korea. Whoa!

I don't mind mixing it up a bit, so I began asking them questions, and we went deep into conversation. I tried hard to find out everything they believed and what they told my neighbor. Once I had done my best to point them back to Scripture and the Jesus found in the Gospels, we parted ways.

As I started up the stairs again, I heard the Lord say, "Go talk to your neighbor about those missionaries. Offer yourself as a guide if she has any questions."

This is interesting, I thought. I really didn't want to do this. She was already solicited about God, the football game was about to start, and I knew this was going to be weird. I was reluctant to do this because I didn't want to meet my neighbor for the first time this way. Furthermore, what if she thinks I am just like those missionaries? I hate the kind of evangelism they do. But I also knew God's voice, and I have seen him use me in ways like this before. So I turned around and went downstairs.

I went up to her door and knocked. The spunky young woman threw open the door and stood there with a puzzled look on her face. She must have thought it was the missionaries back for more.

In that moment I felt the adrenaline rush I always feel when I have just stepped into a faith discussion with someone I don't know. I feel an odd mix of insecurity and certainty: I wonder if I should even be there and how crazy I must look, yet I feel sure God has a plan for this person and wants to talk to him or her through me. I am typically both excited for the life-changing conversation that could ensue and nervous about completely bombing and looking like an idiot.

I simply opened my mouth and started talking. "I overheard you talking to those crazy missionaries a few minutes ago. I talked to them after they left your place. Let me tell you that what they have to say is not from God, and I think it is a bunch of crap."

We both laughed nervously. I realized what I said was pretty intense. Way to say hello first, Beau!

"Here's my point," I quickly continued. "The reason I stopped by is because my wife and I work on the college campus—San Diego State—right up the road. We love helping college students think about God and get their questions answered. I wanted to let you know that if you have any questions about God and faith, you should talk to us, not those weird missionary dudes. We would love to have you over for dinner sometime just to talk, if you would like."

She responded without a pause, "What do you think about gay people?"

Say what?

Evangelism Is Awkward

I will finish the story a little later, but this is a great time to pause to admit that evangelism can be extremely unnerving. Following Jesus can get us into some crazy situations. Take my encounter. Within thirty minutes I was talking about the end of the world, Jesus in Korea and what I thought about homosexuality. I didn't sign up for that, and I am sure you don't wake up most days eagerly antici-pating those types of conversations. They can be incredibly strange, uncomfortable and confusing.

Let's be even more honest. Most of the time, you wouldn't even hear God tell you to wait for the missionaries, let alone go back and talk to the woman. You would more likely blow right by, thinking, *That poor girl. I hope those missionaries don't come to my house!* The problem is that we often don't hear God, or when we do hear him, we opt out. Instead of continuing down the evan-gelism freeway, we take the nearest exit.

> **We often don't hear God, or when we do hear him, we opt out.**

The reality is, however, that in my en-counter, and many of yours, God intends to use us in evangelistic ways. We know this because since the beginning of Genesis we see God on mission to return a fallen creation to relationship with him. Not only is he on mission but he calls everyday people to follow him and advance that mission—people with no training and no development. I especially think about the woman at the well in John 4 and the demoniac in Mark 5. They both returned to their villages without training and spoke out about Jesus! Many came to believe in him because of the testimony of these two. Every one of us is also called to share our faith in Christ and to be a witness.

For a few chapters now I have been encouraging you to share your faith and to be open to God leading you into encounters with your friends. At this point you may be wondering about the role of "gifted" evangelists. Isn't sharing the gospel and leading people to faith in Christ their job?

God has given us five primary callings: apostle, prophet, evangelist, shepherd and teacher. People with these callings are uniquely designed to carry out their vocation. There are gifted evangelists, and we see this clearly in Ephesians 4.

Called evangelists do a few things. First, they equip the church to share the gospel of Jesus. Ephesians 4:12 says God gifted them to "equip his people for works of service, so that the body of Christ may be built up." Another role gifted evangelists play is preaching for conversion. We have seen this clearly through the ministry of Billy Graham, and we continue to see it today in our various networks. Gifted evangelists preach in a way that helps people come to faith in Christ.

But every person is called to be a witness and to share his or her faith. You are called by God to take responsibility for the people around you that are searching and need further understanding. Yes, there are gifted evangelists who can help and will lead many to Christ, but you have a unique responsibility as a follower of Jesus to step into the mission as well. If you have gifted evangelists in your church, I would encourage you to identify them so you and the church know who they are, and ask them to coach you as a witness. They can't reach the people you are designed to reach, but they can coach you, equip you, pray with you and even sometimes go with you.

We cannot opt out of this part of following Jesus just because it feels uncomfortable or we are tempted to put it on the shoulders of someone more gifted.

Look at how many times I could have opted out of the conversation if I had wanted. First, I could have gone upstairs when I saw the missionaries talking to my neighbor. Second, I could have ended sooner my conversation with the missionaries. Third, I could have called it a day when I was done talking with them. I didn't want to talk with them. Neither did I want to knock on my neighbor's door after the missionaries had just talked with her.

But the Spirit told me to do all of these things, and I have learned to obey and follow his directions. So I made the choice to put myself into that nerve-racking situation. I chose to follow God into conversation with the missionaries without any plan of my own. I chose to knock on my neighbor's door, unrehearsed and hoping the words would come out right, which they didn't. I was awkward. The situation was awkward. There was no way around it, though, because God had asked me to step into it. I know God's voice. I had seen many previous moments when God moved in people's lives because of my obedience to his promptings. I couldn't say no because I knew God was up to something. I was so familiar with his whisper that I knew he was instigating something I didn't want to miss. It was a John 2 moment. Plus, I knew one more thing that will set the tone from here on out: *Awkwardness usually precedes God moving in a powerful way.*

Most of the time when God asks us to talk to someone in his name, it will be awkward at some point. But right after some of the initial tension is released, some kind of breakthrough comes, whether in the other person, in us or in the conversation.

Evangelistic moments will freak us out. But if we bail out early we will miss the breakthrough moment that God, the other person and we were longing for the whole time.

The reality is that most people don't do evangelism because they don't want to make others uncomfortable, they don't want to feel pushy, or they anticipate being caught without words in the moment. So people don't even start, or they bail at the first sign of trouble.

Our ego gets in the way. In these moments we are thinking more highly of ourselves than we ought to. We all need an ego check here. It is important to ask ourselves regularly, *Am I tempted to chicken out because of how I might look or feel, or is this genuinely a bad time to bring up Jesus?*

The overwhelming reality in sharing our faith, however, is that most of the encounters God sets up will be unnerving and uncomfortable. There was no way my sticking around to talk to the missionaries wasn't going to be a little crazy. There sure wasn't any way I could knock on my neighbor's door without raising an eyebrow on her face and putting a few butterflies in my stomach.

So again, why didn't I simply head upstairs? And why should you even bother with evangelism?

You do it because you know it may be awkward now, but God is going to move in the next moment. You do it because you know you will have a front-row seat as God goes to work into someone's life.

If you want to see God move, then you need to enter into the awkwardness.

My Neighbor's Breakthrough

Right after my neighbor asked me what I thought about gay people, I put my heart back in my chest and then quickly gathered my thoughts.

"Well, I think God loves gay people," I responded. "He has a lot to say to them, just like he has a lot to say to straight people."

"Oh," she said. "That is a pretty good answer. You see, my sister is gay, and my dad is a fundamentalist Christian. I don't believe what he believes, and I don't go to church. I have lots of questions, but I can't talk to someone who hates gay people."

I assured her my wife and I don't hate gay people, even if we may disagree with sexually active gays about what the Bible has to say about sexuality. I assured her that figuring out that issue would be much easier if she got to know Jesus and see what he had to say himself. I then asked her if she liked to read, which she affirmed. I then loaned her a couple books I thought could be helpful.

Over the next few months my wife and I took our neighbor to a discovery Bible study at our church, had spiritual conversations with her and saw her grow in her faith. She ended up moving shortly after that. She had not accepted Christ, but I saw her grow toward Jesus.

If I would have been categorically against out-of-the-box moments and feeling uncomfortable in evangelism, I would have
missed this opportunity God set up for her. God wants to have an
intimate relationship with her, and I am so thankful I allowed him
to put me in a few intimidating conversations to jump-start her
journey with him. I could have let self-consciousness derail me. I
could have bailed out of the uneasiness. But I didn't, and I got to
see breakthrough, and so did she.

The best evangelists are not devoid of feelings of inadequacy or
fear—quite the contrary. Effective evangelists remind themselves
that awkwardness precedes God moving in others' lives. They learn
to engage it and welcome it. They know that breakthrough is
coming, and they don't want to miss it. They know God is seeking
to save those who are lost. They know the Father is drawing people
to Jesus regularly. They know the harvest is plentiful. They welcome
moments that have the potential to psych them out, so they can see
God move and deliver his people.

Awkward Moments Lead to Breakthroughs

The funny thing about awkward moments is that you and I have them
all the time. Not just in sharing our faith, but in dating relationships,
marriage, at work with our boss and even with friends. I would make
the case that those tense moments often are the way we pass through
a certain threshold to gain more intimacy in our relationships.[1]

> **Tense moments often are
> the way we pass through
> a certain threshold to
> gain more intimacy.**

I remember the first time I revealed
my feelings of attraction to the woman
who is now my wife. I was nervous and
scared because I didn't know if she
would reciprocate. Previously, I had told
other women I liked them and asked
them to date me, and they rejected me on the spot. Not fun. The
moment of tension that surrounds revealing your feelings to
someone for the first time is so thick you could cut it with a knife.

You feel angst because there is a great probability of rejection. But if the person responds positively and is as excited as you, there is great joy, and the relationship goes to deeper places. A new intimacy is created. First, however, there is an awkward moment that has to be passed through.

Sharing our faith is no different. Incredible tension comes into play with people we know God wants us to talk to about Jesus. We are nervous and scared because we don't know if it will be weird or pushy or uncomfortable. We don't want to alienate them, and we don't want to get rejected.

But some of the time when we pop that question, *Would you ever want to talk about faith?* there is an incredible response at the end. They end up being like my downstairs neighbor and actually want to talk about and seek God. It is an astonishing feeling. The uneasy moment precedes a breakthrough experience.

I didn't push my neighbor away in that moment. Could I have? Sure, I guess I could have. But God used it as a way to bring us closer—to grow our relationship and to bring us to a deeper place. In this case, and with many cases of people in our lives, awkward tension brought us closer because we were willing to walk through that threshold and engage the moment.

What makes things awkward? Why are certain situations awkward, and why do we avoid them? The genesis of awkwardness is social rules being broken. The more social rules that are broken, the more awkward encounters become. There are three main social norms we have to break repeatedly if we are going to share our faith, and because we have to break them, most of us don't share—our convictions remain private.

1. Don't talk to strangers. It is not socially acceptable in Western culture to start conversations with people we don't know. Obviously this differs depending on where we live, but for the most part it is a social rule that when we are in public and we don't know someone, we should keep to ourselves. Total strangers generally do not strike up conversations on a plane, train, bus or at the beach.

2. Don't do things that make anyone feel uncomfortable. Our culture is becoming more and more conditioned to comfort. If something doesn't feel good, don't do it. It is not normal to "press through" things that don't feel good. It is normal to avoid them, get rid of them and do something different.

3. Don't press people about what is true or real. It is not okay in our culture, especially the more experience-based it becomes, to act like only one way is right or to even challenge people on what is true or real. We live in a relativistic culture which embraces the mantra "What is good for you is good for you, and what is good for me is good for me."

So any kind of encounter that presses us to break one of these rules will create awkward tension. When we break all three rules—talk to a stranger, make someone feel uncomfortable, and press the person on what is true or real—then we are on our way to a tense moment.

We want to be socially acceptable, which makes it hard to be a bold witness. We want to fit in and not be disruptive. But the reality of being a follower of Jesus is that he asks us to be his witnesses, and this often means breaking one or more of those social rules. Later I will discuss how we can learn to live in this tension, but for now it is enough to be aware of why we avoid awkwardness and how being socially appropriate in public tends to control us.

The Great Commission and the mandate to evangelize the world violate many of these social mores. "Go everywhere" as opposed to knowing your place, "make disciples" as opposed to minding your own business and making the conversation pleasant, and "teach them to obey my commands" as opposed to religious and behavioral liberty.

To illustrate this a bit further, let's turn our attention to a helpful exercise.

Right Next to Scared Is Excited

I frequently train groups in evangelism in churches and on college campuses. I start with an opening exercise that is both fun and revealing. Feel free to get a pen and a piece of paper to do this exercise yourself.

Imagine you are going for a walk in your neighborhood. You stop to say a quick prayer, "God speak to me. I'm listening." Imagine God saying, "Walk one street over." Write down how this feels.

After much thought, you decide God was speaking to you and you head one street over. Record how this feels.

Imagine that a house sticks out to you for some reason. You sense God saying, "Go, stand near the house." Write down how this feels.

As you approach the house, two people walk into the front yard; they are talking about relationship with God. You sense God wants you to ask them, "Do you understand who God is and how to have a relationship with him?" Record how this feels.

They reply, "Not really. That's what we are trying to figure out. What do you mean?" How does this feel?

You then ask them if you can explain what it looks like to have a relationship with Jesus. How does it feel to ask them this? Write it down.

They say they would love to know. Record how this feels.

You explain the good news of Jesus, and they decide they want to accept Jesus into their lives. They thank you profusely for taking the time to interrupt their day to explain this to them. You invite them to your church home group, get their contact info and leave. Write down how this makes you feel.

When I lead this exercise, I ask a few people to read their lists aloud. Their lists often look like this:

- Weird!
- This is interesting.

- Heart pumping and weird.
- Awkward.
- Really awkward.
- Scared.
- Excited!
- Pumped!

The list gets pretty dicey in the middle. But right after the word *scared* we see the word *excited*. Right next to it! If you recall nothing else, please remember that right after *awkward* and *scared* is *excited*. I tell my seminar groups every time that awkwardness always precedes God breaking through to the person. Staying through the weird moments will allow you to watch God work in the exciting moments afterward.

> **Staying through the weird moments will allow you to watch God work in the exciting moments afterward.**

Good evangelists aren't skilled enough, trained enough or cool enough to avoid moments when they feel underprepared and out of control. They go through them. Nevertheless, they stay engaged and trust that God has something coming. This is what makes them different.

Later, I will address knowing the difference between awkward moments that come from God and your own pushiness. There is a difference. But for now you need to know that God sets up weird evangelistic situations, and you have to go through them if you want to see your friends, family, neighbors, coworkers and even strangers transformed by Christ. If you want *scared* to meet *excited*, you have to stay the course with God.

It grieves me that many people do not get to see God move because they bailed out at step four or five in the exercise, and they never progressed to steps seven and eight. I want that to never happen. Instead, I want us to be bold in those awkward and fearful moments. I want everyone to learn to anticipate God's movement and have a front-row seat to see his work. I want you to enjoy many people saying yes to Jesus. There is no greater experience than seeing people turn their lives over to Jesus and having them thank you for connecting them to their eternal Father.

Bad Awkward and Good Awkward

At this point you may be thinking, *I know a lot of evangelists who share the Word of God, and they are weird! Those guys make it look awful.*

The last thing I want to do is empower annoying or pushy evangelists to keep doing what they are doing. I realize those people exist. At times we can be like that if we're not careful. We all totally embarrass ourselves in different moments. I am not suggesting we justify those encounters and say, "Oh well, God is still working." There is a difference between being creepy and the tense moments set up by God.

Lenses of discernment. Two important lenses can help us discern whether an awkward moment is from God or if we are creating it ourselves.

There is a difference between being creepy and the tense moments set up by God.

1. Sense God's call. If you are clear that God has invited you into a moment, any awkwardness during that encounter undoubtedly is part of the God moment. When we create our own moments and force ourselves into situations, it's likely we are creating the tension. It's important to remember that with my downstairs neighbor I was responding to what was already happening with the missionaries. I didn't force my way into something that wasn't already happening. I had a strong sense that God was inviting me into this moment. My action was not coming from my desire to make something happen.

For those who are on the bolder side, do a double take and ask God if he is inviting you into this moment or you are forcing it. For the majority of you who stay far away from awkwardness, don't write God off simply because it feels outlandish.

2. *Look for openness.* When God is up to something, you won't need to push. You will be invited in.

Again, with my neighbor, I sensed God asking me to knock on her door. Once I did, she was very engaging and welcoming. She asked questions and wanted to talk. Yes, I had to initiate, but no, I did not have to push.

If you have to be forceful, *you* are creating the awkwardness. God is a gentleman and doesn't barge in.

If you sense that God is inviting you to take a risk and the person is responding, though it may be awkward, go for it, because God is in it!

Let me share two stories that should help you understand the difference between being weird and diving into an awkward moment set up by God.

Bad awkward: "Want to join our revolution?" When I first began working with InterVarsity, I attended a meeting with all the staff in our area. One day our task was to practice a new gospel presentation and then go out in pairs to share it on campus. Even though I had shared my faith hundreds of times before, I wasn't exactly smooth with the new model we were learning.

One of the conversations my partner and I got into was definitely strange, like many are, but this was different. The guys we were talking to were not open to us. Every time we asked them a question, they halfheartedly answered as if they couldn't wait to get away from us. Unfortunately, I kept pushing and finally got one of them to say we could share our message with them.

I launched into this new gospel presentation, but when I got to the part about Jesus bringing healing to the world and how we get to join him in his mission, I froze. Lost for words, I said the strangest thing possible: "We are wondering if you want to join our revolution. You can do this thing with Jesus too!"

As soon as I said "want to join our revolution?" I knew I was being a creep. So did my partner. I'm pretty sure the guys thought I was starting a cult. They said "No, thanks" and hurried off.

As my partner and I walked back to debrief with everyone else, all we could talk about was how disturbing I was. We were bummed that I scared the guys off.

I don't really know what caused me to do it. I do know it was a situation where I was plain awkward and God had little to do with it.

Obviously, I didn't use the second lens. These people were not engaging me and were not inviting me in. I did not read the cues correctly, and if I could have done it over again, I would have shut the conversation down much earlier, sensing that they were not open. Though I sensed God inviting me to share the gospel with people that day, I also needed to pay attention to how each individual was responding and act accordingly.

Good awkward: "I am a stripper." Sometimes awkwardness is harder to decipher.

One day my friend Matt and I decided to say a quick prayer in the car before we went into the mall. The prayer went something like this: "God, if you have anyone for us to talk to while we are here, we are open—just show us who." Just then, a lowrider pulled into the parking ramp and stopped near us. Two guys who looked like they could be in a gang were bumping music. Matt looked right at me with a long face and said in a dejected voice, "Ugh, I think we need to talk to them." He wasn't scared of the guys, but he was embarrassed and feeling out of place. He didn't want to walk up to two guys in the parking structure and bring up Jesus. But he had felt the nudge from God, so we went up to them as they got out of their car (totally creepy, right?) and asked them if they had a moment to talk about God.

One of the guys quickly said, "No, we don't have time, man." But the other quietly said, "Sure."

Matt introduced us and asked them what they did for a living. One of them answered, "I am a stripper." To this day, I can't remember what the other guy answered.

Matt remained composed, stayed the course and started to give his testimony. Matt has a great testimony and is good at sharing the story of Jesus. When he finished, he asked the guys what they thought and if either one of them wanted to pray and accept Jesus into their lives.

Again, one guy declined, but the other said, "I would like to!"

Matt and I were caught off-guard, but we bowed our heads and prayed with him to accept Christ and experience forgiveness for his sins.

We went our separate ways after that. There is no telling how those guys turned out. Matt and I wondered who would follow up with them, but in the end we knew we obeyed God and were confident he set up that encounter. We did what we could and were jazzed about seeing God move in such an unexpected way, especially when we felt so unsettled and wanted to quit.

If Matt had listed his feelings for each step of the encounter, he certainly would have included the word *awkward*, but it would have been followed by *excited*. Matt felt like a dork the whole way through that encounter. Until, that is, the guy said he wanted to accept Christ. It was a powerful moment for Matt and me, one we still marvel at a decade later. It helped me understand that hair-raising moments are sometimes necessary in order to see God's plans carried out.

> **Hair-raising moments are sometimes necessary in order to see God's plans carried out.**

This is a great example of a tense and uncomfortable moment, but clearly it was of God. How do I know this? First, Matt sensed God calling him into this situation. He already felt awkward and wasn't looking for the opportunity to talk with them. But God was speaking as we were praying, and it was clear to us that God was inviting us into the moment. When God calls us forward, we can be confident the awkwardness is part of the spiritual encounter. Second, one of the guys kept inviting us further in. He wanted to know more. So we kept going.

Key Step: Finding Your Neighbor

The encounter with my downstairs neighbor is not unique to me. You too have people like her living near you. But you won't know it unless you keep an ear open to God's leading and an eye open to seeing your neighbors. God is waiting to send you into some sticky situations that you may miss if you don't realize he is calling. God is not beyond awkward moments, and my prayer is that you will respond to him next time he calls.

Reflection Questions

1. Think about a recent time you felt awkward. Describe your feelings.

2. What do you dislike about feeling awkward?

3. How do you avoid awkward situations? What defense mechanisms do you use?

4. As you read this chapter, who came to mind?

5. Is there something or someone God's been calling you to that you've been ignoring because it could be awkward to take the first step?

4

They're Experience Based

ONE DAY WHEN I WAS ON CAMPUS having coffee with a seeking student, he said something that helped me see much deeper into the experience-based person's soul. "I am not concerned with what you think is true or not, Beau. I want to know if this works. Is the Christian faith relevant to my life?"

I was walking him through *Mere Christianity* and trying to convince him that Jesus was the one true God. It wasn't working for him. I was frustrated because I love this book and couldn't believe it wasn't convincing to him. But even more, I was frustrated that I wasn't being effective; I didn't know how to reach this student. I was thinking to myself, *I am showing you how this works!* None of my tactics were working.

I came to realize that I was trying to answer the wrong question. Once I understood that the main question people are asking today is different from twenty years ago, I was able to move past the frustration and think about how to actually help. If you were born before 1980 and have had evangelism training, your training most likely answered questions people were asking in earlier generations. But today's culture is asking different questions. Therefore we need to start from different places and use some different models. In this chapter I will present a different approach.

Part of the reason evangelism feels awkward is that most people today are experience based, but the evangelism training you received is reason based. The evangelistic methods you are equipped with don't match today's culture. Hence, you're not connecting in many conversations, and evangelism may be starting to feel "old school." By *old school* I mean that you may be saying things like "Evangelism just doesn't work today. It may have worked before, but it's too pushy in this culture. I don't want to be pushy."

I am not suggesting that previous models were wrong or that they don't work at all today. But we need alternative models to better reach people in an experience-based culture. Culture is changing; our call to witness is not. We can't throw the baby out with the bath water. Cultural methods may need to go, but the Great Commission is permanent.

The Experience-Based Philosophy

> **Culture is changing; our call to witness is not.**

We are living in an increasingly experience-oriented culture. These people (millennials, postmoderns or Generation Y) generally base truth on their experiences, on what makes sense for their life. More pointedly, they are asking, "Does this work? Is this real?" while previous generations asked, "Is this true?"

The fundamental starting point, therefore, is different. Thirty years ago we used evangelism tactics like the Four Spiritual Laws, the bridge diagram, the Romans Road or the evidence for the resurrection. (The Romans Road, in a nutshell, teaches the truths of Romans 3:23; 5:8; 6:23; 10:9-19, although there are several variations. If you're not familiar with the others, you can find them through a Google search.) All great stuff. But all of them *try to convince someone that Christianity is true.* It worked well in a culture that was more cognitive and rationalistic.

People who embrace modernity, in contrast to postmoderns, want to be convinced of what is true, and when they are convinced *intellectually,* they will change their *behavior.* But experience-based people are the opposite. They need to be convinced that something works, not that it is true. Once they are shown that this faith is real—makes a difference—for their life, they will change their behavior and eventually their mind.

There are benefits and disadvantages to sharing the gospel in each culture. Because people from reason-based cultures are convinced that universal truth exists, they will engage in vigorous debate about whether Christianity is true. If we can convince them that Scripture is right, they will change their mind and believe. The problem is that the experiential side of faith is often ignored, and following Jesus can become primarily about belief and not so much about behavior. Faith and action are divorced.

However, rigorous debate and convincing truths about Christ are not the most compelling ways to reach experience-based people. Their eyes glaze over five minutes into this kind of presentation. Truth isn't their starting point. So trying to reach today's young people with approaches that worked years ago can be frustrating.

For example, in my witnessing experience, people entrenched in an experience-based worldview often balk at the idea of Christ being the only way to God. Why? Because they imagine people they love not being with them in heaven. They then default to the adage, "What is good for you is good for you, and what is good for me is good for me—whatever works." Of course I am generalizing here, but the majority of people I talk with today live in this reality. It is hard for our present culture to accept that Christianity is *the* way. It breaks their rules of respect and tolerance for other people's experience. (I am not saying we shouldn't present Christ as central but that the way we go about doing so must change.)

If we lead with propositional truths or convincing arguments and people are not responding, it would be easy to write them off as hardhearted. But this may not be the case. The advantage of witnessing to experience-based people is that they are much more open to seeking and don't see things as black or white, right or wrong. They are curious and much more open. They want to know what works and whether a certain community of faith makes life meaningful. They are more open to the mystical and supernatural side of faith. Postmodern people want to talk, share experience and learn about life together. They want to serve the community and bring healing to the city. They want to experience faith and see how it makes life work better. In a sense they want to *act* their way into faith, while previous generations needed to *think* their way in. This is why many missional churches are moving toward decentralized and experiential models of faith, where groups meet in neighborhoods, pubs, campuses and work environments.

While many have been tempted to write off this next generation as godless because they are so hard to reach, I would suggest we don't understand them very well, and we need a new approach. Their worldview is not better or worse than previous worldviews. It's simply different, and we need to start from a different place with this different culture.

Understanding these worldview differences changed the way I share my faith with experience-based people. It also changed the way I train people to witness, and how I run the ministry God entrusted to me.

So what can we do to reach this culture, and how can we rightly and fully share the gospel with experience-based people?

We Need A Different Model

When trying to figure out how to reach our experience-based culture, I providentially came across the Celtic model of evangelism.[1] The Celtic model emphasizes process and journey, which fits well with today's culture. St. Patrick developed this model as he reached out to the Celtic people, and it stands in contrast to the "persuasion" or "Roman" model that dominated evangelism during his time. If we want to reach today's culture, it will help to move toward the Celtic model and away from the persuasion model (see fig. 4.1).

Persuasion Model	Celtic Model
1. Persuasion evangelism	1. Incarnation evangelism
2. Proclamation	2. Soul awakening
3. Conversion	3. Community
4. Community	4. Transformation

Fig. 4.1. Process of conversion

The Celtic model. The Celtic model emphasizes incarnation, living among the people and awakening them to Jesus through relationship, discussion and preaching. Once people awaken to the reality of God, they will join the community. In other words, they "belong before they believe." Later, as they come to faith in Christ through study and classes, they will be challenged toward whole-life transformation.

Being with people and then helping them belong to community before believing or changing anything is the Celtic model. This is helpful for experience-based people because they need to see if it is real before they believe and change their behavior. They want to see if this gospel we talk about has power to actually transform broken lives. John Wesley, who furthered this model and developed it into Methodism, was very comfortable allowing people to belong before they believed, and as they came to see that Christ is true, they would change their minds and their lives.

The persuasion model. The persuasion model is very different. The emphasis is on persuading people to believe what is true about God. It focuses on first changing minds and then experiencing community. Institutions of the persuasion model often use an up-front preacher to issue a call to faith and challenge people to change their beliefs. Once the person converts to Christ, he or she is encouraged to join the community.

We see this model in our churches and most famously in the Billy Graham crusades. People are first convinced of the saving grace of

Christ (believing) and then encouraged to attend church (belonging). This is a terrific way to convert people that want explanations and are convinced by the truth.

To be clear, there is nothing wrong with this model. It has worked for centuries and still works today with some people. I still use it and prefer it in some situations. But if we are going to reach a generation of experience-oriented people, we need to use a different model, one in which our evangelistic efforts and church structures first help people belong to community and then experience Christ. We need to emphasize process and journey more than persuasion and truth.

Analogy of a house. To illustrate this further, let's think about a house as an analogy for the experience-based person. If the front door of our evangelism efforts with modern people is to "convince them of what is true," then it makes perfect sense that we would start with persuasion, whether through the bridge diagram or proofs of the resurrection. As the seeker rings the doorbell of faith, we would answer and start persuading with the truth. Our first encounter with friends or neighbors would be to convince them that Jesus is God. We might use a tract or a set of propositional truths to do so.

But today the front-door greeting needs to change. As the experience-based person rings the doorbell of faith, we need to answer the door and greet them with a personal story. They need to hear how God is moving in our life and how this faith in Christ works. They are asking a different question: "Does Christianity (or Jesus) work?"

The Front Door: Transformational Stories

Today, the best way to start a discussion with seekers is to tell them stories of transformation, to let them into your life to see that Jesus is real to you and is transforming your life. Let me be clear here. I am not suggesting that we tell them stories to show how Jesus is "adding on to" our life but that he is changing us and making us whole.

When I am driving in the car with a friend and he asks me, "So what does it mean for me to have a relationship with God?" I don't

Today, the best way to start a discussion with seekers is to tell them stories of transformation.

start with the Romans Road to convince him that he is a sinner and that Jesus can save him. I will get there, but this is not the front door. Instead, I will tell him a story of how Jesus is working in my life relationally.

For example, I had a friend who struggled with anger. When he asked me how to have a relationship with God, I said, "Well, Bill, relationship with God works like this *for me:* You know how you struggle with anger, and you have been telling me how you wish you could change? Well, I struggle with anger too, and the other day I got overly mad at my wife. It was wrong, and I felt bad about it. Having Jesus in my life allows me to be in relationship with a powerful and loving God who can change me and help me work the way I was intended to work. Having the power of God through relationship with Christ allows me to pray to him and ask him to change my character, to make me less angry. Having access to the love of God allows me to read about him in Scripture and learn to follow his ways of loving people. Jesus is my compass, and I am reorienting my life around his directions. That is how faith in Christ works. That is how it is real for me. That is how my relationship with God works."

When Bill becomes more curious about the reality of faith in Jesus, who transforms lives, I will then move Bill to the "living room" for the next part of the discussion.

The Living Room: Scripture Study

When people are intrigued with my faith life or curious about Jesus and ask more questions about how it all works, I invite them into Scripture study so they can see the words of Jesus for themselves. While experience-based people don't want to be preached at, they are very open to discussing and learning about

God. So doing powerful interactive Scripture studies with
them is essential. I see many
people come to faith in Jesus
through Scripture studies. This is
where I can talk about profound

truths of God through relational and authentic conversation.

Models of conversion. When it comes to helping people come
to Christ and follow him, it is helpful to consider a few models.[2]

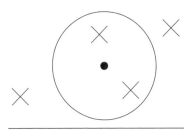

Fig 4.2. Bounded-set model

The model we are most used
to in evangelism is the
bounded-set model. In this
model there is clear distinction
between who is in and who is
out. The key question is, "Are
you in or are you out?" This is
what leads to evangelism

tactics such as the Four Spiritual Laws, or the bridge diagram, or
even questions like, "If you died tonight, would you go to heaven?"
The bounded-set model is of course biblical and we see this very
clearly through the encounter of Saul in Acts. We can point to the
exact moment when he "converted."

Another model of con-
version is the centered set.
The key question here is, "Are
you moving toward the center
or away from it?" In a culture
where people are experience-
based and need to belong
before they believe, this is a

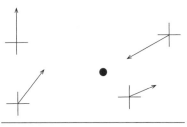

Fig 4.3. Centered-set model

helpful question to be asking and a helpful model to have in mind.
This is the model that I tend to orient my ministry around today
and is the basis for much of the writing in this chapter.

We see this model prevalent in the Gospels, where people are moving closer or farther away from Jesus. Sinners seem to draw near, and the Pharisees seem to draw away as their hearts become harder and harder. Furthermore, we can't pinpoint exactly when someone like Peter had his "conversion" moment. There seem to be many moments along the way. This is how many people in our culture experience Jesus today, and it is helpful to be able to frame ministry around structures and conversations that help people move closer toward Jesus.

When we talk about people having an *awakening moment,* this is a great picture to show them to help them see how their moment with God was one in which they are drawing near, and that they can continue to seek him and take steps toward Jesus. You can explain that joining a small group is a great place to belong before they actually believe. The community is designed to help people move closer to Jesus.

But if people make a decision and are actually having a *believing moment,* then I want to help them understand the bounded-set model and the realities of being "in Christ" and inside the kingdom of God. It is important for them to realize that one actually can be "in Christ" and not just always journeying toward him. Your life can be hidden with him, and you can have access to his infinite power available through his resurrection (Ephesians 1:19). But that decision also lends itself to another model and question that I find very helpful in evangelism—especially for discipling a new believer just after conversion.

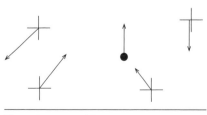

This model is the *journey model,* and the main question you are asking here is, "Are you following in the footsteps of the leader or not?"

Once people have a *be-*

Fig 4.4. Journey model

lieving moment and declare to you that they want to surrender their life to Jesus, I find it helpful to explain to them that being a follower of Christ means submitting our lives to him as Lord, allowing him full access to speak into all parts of our lives to bring transformation and sanctification. We are called to now follow Jesus in all areas of life. Asking the question above is helpful.

Jesus stories. I always start with Jesus stories. Picking narratives in which Jesus interacts with another person are the most helpful. Again, the person I'm sharing with is experiential, so showing how Jesus "works" in another's life is essential. In InterVarsity we practice this in what we call GIGs (Groups Investigating God). The following are two of my favorite stories.

The prodigal son (Luke 15:11-32). The key idea behind this story is that God will always accept us back no matter what we do—even if we have been acting like he is dead. The key questions I ask are (1) Where are you in this story: far away, turning around or coming back? This helps people figure out where they currently are with God and to put themselves into the story. (2) How can God accept the prodigal back without punishment? This allows me to tell them the deep truth of substitutionary atonement and that Christ took the punishment we deserve. The reason Jesus is able to tell this story about a loving and accepting father is that he knew he was going to the cross to take the punishment the son deserved!

The calling of Levi (Luke 5:27-32). The key idea behind this narrative is that Jesus wants all kinds of people to follow him. Even the most messed-up people who do evil. Jesus makes it clear that he is a physician and that he came to heal those that are sick. The key questions I ask are (1) What kind of things do you think are broken in your life? (2) How open are you to letting Jesus fix them? This allows me to get to the truth that we cannot follow Jesus if we don't see our brokenness and allow him to fix it. Jesus is not an add-on to our current life but the healer who has come to transform us into new life.

Studying Scripture together is powerful. I literally print out the story and bring a few markers to the coffee shop. I'll then ask the person to take five minutes to mark up the story, saying, "Circle or underline things that stand out to you, and write down questions that you have." Then we talk about the story, and I lead the person to the main point and ask a key question. It is here, in the context of relationship, with trust built, with Scripture in front of us, that I am able to proclaim the gospel clearly and powerfully. Like I said, I see many people turn to Christ through GIGs.[3]

Of course I share propositional truths with seekers, but I don't lead with them. I lead with story—my story and Jesus' stories. Then I work propositional truths into the conversation. For example, with the prodigal son, I talk about the wayward son and discuss how we all run from God. I then bring up some Scripture, doctrine or propositional truth, such as, "All have sinned and fall short of the glory of God" (Romans 3:23).

It's not that we can't have deep theological talks or use convincing arguments with experience-based people. But I'm suggesting that we start with story first to build trust and help seekers better answer their primary question: Does this work?

After we have our deep conversation in the living room, it is time for them to move to the upstairs portion of the faith conversation.

Upstairs: Life Change

Once we have shared our transformational stories and talked through Scripture with the seeker, we need to make clear one more thing to an experience-based person: Life change is essential to following Jesus.

Life change is essential to following Jesus.

Because these people generally are relativists (they believe truth is subjective), it is easy for them to "believe" something but not act on it. They can hold disparate beliefs and use whichever one makes sense (or feels comfortable) for them at the moment. This is a terrible problem for following Christ. It's why we see people make decisions to follow Jesus at church or gospel rallies, but then not change their lifestyle to conform to what they say they believe. They had a powerful experience that was real that day, but they added Jesus on to their previous set of beliefs. They didn't let Jesus take absolute center. So when they aren't "feeling" it much anymore or they have a bad day, they change which truth to follow. Jesus isn't "working" anymore.

In 2007 I realized that most of the people who stood at our campus fellowship meeting to declare they wanted to follow Christ weren't following him a few months later. This frustrated me. More importantly, it made me ask why. I realized that though they were experiencing Christ at these meetings, discipleship and life change did not accompany them as they continued forward.

Awakening Moment Versus Believing Moment

From that point on I made sure that we met with every person who made a decision for Christ to ask them, "Do you think you had an awakening moment last night or a believing moment?" We defined these terms for them as follows:

- *Awakening moment.* You sensed something of God in the service—a powerful testimony, moving music and verses—or you resonated with something the speaker said. You stood up because you are awakening to God's presence, but you are not ready yet to follow Jesus and let him call the shots in your life. You want to seek him out and learn more first.

- *Believing moment.* You have come to a point in your journey where you realize following Jesus is more than experiences. It is about letting him transform you and call the shots in your life. You realize that he has died for your sin, buried it in the grave and risen to give you new life and purpose in this world. You are saying yes to him driving your life and being in control.

Ninety percent of people who stood up said it was an awakening moment. So I would tell them, "That is great! God did a powerful thing last night in your life, and he is getting your attention. What you need to do now is continue in a GIG and keep studying the life of Jesus. You are not yet ready to call yourself a follower of Jesus. Following Jesus means you are willing to let him call the shots in your life and bring change to the areas you don't want to change but he says you need to. Then you are ready to make Jesus God—the center of your life." Then I would usher them back to the living room for more Scripture study and community.

But for those who were ready to follow Jesus, our discussion immediately became about life change. Experience-based, relativistic people show us that Jesus is truth when they are willing to orient their lives around him. Until they are willing to change their life around Jesus' teaching, we should be concerned whether they are truly following him or if he is another add-on to make them feel happy.

> **Experience-based, relativistic people show us that Jesus is truth when they are willing to orient their lives around him.**

Gospel conversations with experience-based people can be fascinating and exciting. There are great opportunities for the gospel in this kind of culture as long as we remember that process needs to lead the way. Hold in one hand your transformational stories; hold Jesus' stories in the other. Learn to tell both your story and Jesus' stories well, and you will go far in leading many people to Christ in today's culture.[4]

Key Step: Show Them

Think of a friend like Bill. How can you show this person that Jesus "works" instead of trying to prove that Jesus is true?

Reflection Questions

1. What do you like about the Celtic model of evangelism? Does it make sense to you for today's culture and the people you know?

2. What strikes you about the analogy of the house with regard to evangelism and the process of conversion?

3. What concerns you and what excites you about the current experience-based culture?

4. Thinking back on your own journey, describe an awakening moment and a believing moment. Reflect on the similarities and the differences between those two moments.

A WITNESS AT WORK
Down the College Road

Nico Gervasoni, president,
Delta Tau Delta fraternity at UCLA

"Even though I am not the most verbal guy in my witness, I do make space for people to explore Jesus." As president of his fraternity Nico Gervasoni started a Bible study so people who are intimidated by church had a place to talk about faith right in the fraternity house.

It is not the easiest experience to be a standout follower of Christ inside a frat house. As you can imagine, the Greek system is known for many things other than Jesus. I love how Nico is a prime example of engaging the awkwardness that can come up so his brothers have a chance to hear the gospel and respond to Jesus.

Recently, through the weekly Bible study and the constant witness of Nico and the team, a fraternity brother of theirs accepted Christ.

"I still get really nervous when it is time for me to be vocal about my faith, and sometimes I shy away, but God is growing me as his witness."

5

You Are in a Spiritual Battle

THINK ABOUT A PERSON whom you long to see come to Christ—that person you have tried to share with, but nothing seems to work. I have a couple of people in my life like that. Sometimes in witness we find ourselves totally stuck and in need of more power than mere words. Sharing the gospel clearly, trying our hardest to convince someone and even sharing our testimony doesn't seem to have enough power. So we feel stuck. One reality that we need to consider, especially in situations like these, is the dynamics of the spiritual realm, namely, the effect spiritual warfare has on witness and the incredible ability for miracles to open seemingly closed people to the gospel—people that for whatever reason will not come to belief in Jesus through our words and sharing alone.

A Miracle Was Needed

When I was a sophomore in college I decided to go on a mission trip to China. It was 2003, the SARS virus hit and the trip was canceled a month before we were supposed to leave. We were rerouted to Kenya, and I started brushing up on Swahili. Then a terrorist attacked the airport, and that trip was canceled a week before we were to leave. Again, we were rerouted—this time to Egypt. The way this trip came together was strange, but nothing surprised me more than what God did in a few days visiting a forgotten village along the desert roads outside Cairo.

Upon arriving in Cairo we met a pastor from Iraq, and one day he asked me and a few of my buddies, "Do you want to come with me next week while I preach in an obscure village?" We were over-eager twenty-year-olds looking for adventure, and we jumped at the chance. The next thing I knew, I was on a bus driving down a dusty road. An Egyptian woman in her fifties stood up in the front and said, "Are you ready to share the gospel?"

My insides sank and I thought to myself, *I am a new Christian and have no idea what I am doing. Plus, we just came to hear this guy preach. We are not part of the plan.*

I was terrified, but I thought of a great excuse. "Excuse me, we were told we were just coming to watch and pray as the pastor preaches. So I didn't even bring a Bible, and I only know one Scripture by memory."

The woman quickly pulled out of her pocket a bright orange Gideons Bible, threw it to me down the long rows of seats and said, "Here, now you have one."

Inside I am dying. I am so scared. I don't know the language or the people, and there are threats to those who share the gospel in closed countries like this. *What the heck am I getting into and why did I sign up for this?*

The woman went on to explain that we each would get an inter-preter, and we would be sent house to house to do three things: share the gospel, pray for people and then invite them to the church service later that night.

The bus arrived at our destination; we hurriedly unloaded, met our translator and hit the road. Literally, I had not been there five minutes, and I was walking down the windy roads of this poor village nervously anticipating sharing the gospel.

The first household we got to was a small family, and they were poor. But they were friendly and generous with food and drink. My eighteen-year-old translator struck up a conversation, and for about thirty minutes they talked in Arabic. I just sat there and did my best to nod and smile—no clue what was going on. Then all of a sudden, the translator turns to me and says, "Okay, share the gospel with them; they are ready."

What? I was not ready for this! Thanks for the warning, man. What am I going to do now? I was panic-stricken; I had nothing to give these people. I did my best to thumb through the flaming orange Gideons Bible, but it was so small I could barely read it. I was able to find Romans and remembered there was something called the Romans Road. I nervously shared the series of Scriptures these people should be aware of: their sin and how they deserve death and punishment for that sin, but God will save them through Jesus. Nice warm-up! They nodded their heads and said thanks. We left quickly. So awkward!

I had no feedback, and now we were on to the next house getting ready to share with that family. I will never forget the moment. It still feels like only yesterday. I prayed as we walked the dirty street, "God, that was weird. I didn't like that, and I know it wasn't effective. You have to give me something, God. I don't understand this translator, I don't understand the people, and I have no way to give them an appropriate message. Please speak to me something for these people."

We got to the next house and entered. The guy was angry, and he was alone. Again, I sat there at the kitchen table as my translator talked with this angry guy. But then something happened that changed my life forever. God spoke to me clear as day. He said, "Someone in this house is sick."

I freaked out because I had never heard God speak to me before. I was new to faith and not in a charismatic church. I couldn't believe what I was hearing, and I was so taken aback by the voice of God that I interrupted my translator!

"Hey, man," I said, as I tapped him on the shoulder. "I know this is weird, but you have to ask this guy if someone in this house is sick. God just told me there is someone sick here."

You should have seen the look on this teenage translator's face. He did not want to ask the guy. But in my bold way, I told him, "Do it, please."

He asked the guy sheepishly if there was anyone sick in the house, and the guy looked like he had seen a ghost. "How do you know that? I never told you that!"

The translator, panicking now, just came right out with it. "God told the American that someone here is sick."

The man calmed down a bit and began to tell us that his wife had just come down with a sickness and that she was in the back room. They did not know what it was. We asked him if we could pray for her, but he did not want us to go back there. So we prayed with him in the kitchen and then went on our way. But before we left, the man, full of joy that God revealed himself in the situation, turned to us and said thank you. When we arrived, he was angry and confused, and as we left he was smiling. God had shown up.

I was shocked. I had no idea how to interpret this, but I quickly remembered a prayer time I had with an older Episcopalian woman before the trip. When I prayed with her, she told me that God wanted to give me the gift of discernment. I had no idea what that meant or when that would be, but in that moment in Egypt I realized that God had given me some kind of supernatural gift.

For the rest of the day, as we visited house after house, God spoke to me words of knowledge and gave me discernment about every family. Literally, as we would walk into the house, a word from God about the residents would hit my mind. It was the wildest thing—something Hollywood might include in a movie script. But it was real! I would get images, words, names of people, and then when I shared them, the people would be shocked and wonder how I knew.

That day God answered my prayers for clarity and help in sharing the gospel. He gave me supernatural power to know things I should not have known. It opened up conversations for the gospel that I would not have been able to have. It brought many people to church that night; the room was filled and people were awakened to Jesus.

A Withered Hand Straightens Out

The next day I went back to the same village full of faith and ready for more. I could not wait to get ahold of what God was giving. It was so much fun to interact with God this way, and even better to see him breaking into others' lives.

One of the last houses we went to on the second day was home to an old couple in their seventies or eighties. The woman had a withered hand and the man was angry and bitter. He was hot, to say the least. As soon as we got to the door, he was yelling about how God had not blessed him, and he was like Job. He was mad at his financial situation. Mad at his wife's health. Mad at everything. And he had good reason to be angry.

Partway through his venting, I asked him if I could pray for his wife's hand. He was unsure about it, but I urged him a bit more and assured him I would be polite and gentle. He agreed, so I moved next to her on a bed across the room. I laid my hands on her wrist, which was hard as rock. Her fingers curled toward her forearm, totally clenched up. I started to pray, and about thirty seconds later I felt something pop and her forearm loosened, kind of like a frozen bag of peas becoming soft and malleable. Her once rock-hard forearm was now thawed. I stopped praying and smoothed her fingers out into full extension. Her hand was now fully stretched out and normal looking.

"Oh my God!" a few of us shockingly exclaimed. I mean, we kind of believed in healing, but we had never seen it before. I was pinching myself. I was so amazed at what I had just seen.

The man's jaw dropped. All he and the woman could say was, "*Al hamdulillah*" ("Praise be to God") over and over.

I still didn't believe it, so I looked for a way to test it. Sitting next to her on a table were two giant glass Coke bottles, the kind that served four to five people. They were a few pounds each, and I asked the old man if before we came his wife could have held one of those in her withered hand. He looked at me exasperated, wondering why I was asking that and muttered, "Of course not." So I grabbed a Coke bottle and jammed it into her hand. She gripped it and held it out like an Olympics trophy. She was proud, we were amazed, and all of us just kept clapping, shouting and repeating "*Al hamdulillah.*"

Later that night the church was packed. Hundreds had come to hear the preacher, and many gave their life to Christ. There was an incredible buzz inside the church and village, and even the pastors called me aside in the middle of the service, asking, "What have you done? We have never seen miracles like this! How are we supposed to respond to the village now that they are expecting Jesus to do this?" I was perplexed at their anxiety, but I also understood that chaos was ensuing. I was just a college sophomore, though, and had no idea what was happening. So I simply reminded them, "Guys, you told me to go out and share the gospel, pray for families and invite them to church. I did that! I don't know why this happening. Jesus is ready to heal more people, obviously."

Sometimes Evangelism Needs to Go Supernatural

In that moment evangelism got supernatural for the pastors and me. None of us were expecting miracles to happen, but they did. The signs and wonders broke through to people who otherwise would not have been open to Jesus. We needed miracles that day in the village, and Jesus provided them. Many were saved, and that trip forever changed the way I thought about evangelism and the need for the supernatural.

I couldn't help but consider how I needed to engage the supernatural from that point forward in evangelism. It no longer was about saying the right thing or delivering the perfect gospel message. Yes, I needed to know how to share the gospel well, and

I worked very hard at that. But this trip showed me that some encounters need power beyond words—a demonstration of the Spirit would be needed.

But most evangelism training I have encountered in the West does not talk about supernatural experiences. It is com-

Some encounters need power beyond words.

posed of slick sayings, cool diagrams and the right Scriptures to convince people to believe. It is almost entirely cognitive and wordy. None of this is wrong. But what if the person we are meeting doesn't need to be convinced to believe something first? What if the person needs to be shown the power of God so he or she can *experience* God first?

We Are Meant for the Supernatural

I think Paul understood this well. He says, "I came to you in weakness with great fear and trembling. My message and my preaching were not with wise and persuasive words, but with a demonstration of the Spirit's power, so that your faith might not rest on human wisdom, but on God's power" (1 Corinthians 2:3-5). Paul didn't want people's faith to rest on human wisdom; he wanted their faith to be based on God's power. That is reason enough to consider leading with the supernatural in witness. And in some cases words will not be enough. Some people need healing, a word of knowledge or a demon cast out before they are open to God. We have to be ready to engage the supernatural side so God can show the seeking person his power.

This is what happened for me in Egypt. I was trained to share the Romans Road and quote the right Scriptures. But in that dusty Egyptian town I needed more. My words weren't enough, and even the Scriptures I was sharing with them they weren't understanding. I was finding myself confused and frustrated because I totally believe in the power of the Word of God. Why was this not working? But once God performed a miracle (gave me a word of knowledge or healing), people opened up and the Scriptures made sense. Jesus was a great interpreter for those miracles, and Scripture was their guide to make sense of it all. They wanted to know this God, and it was easy to point to Scripture and say, "Jesus is the one you want."

So why are we so uncomfortable going here with God? Why does the idea of engaging people with the supernatural side of God make so many squirm in our culture? Why is it so weird, taboo, spooky and only for wackos?

Jordan Seng addresses this in his book *Miracle Work*:

> Supernatural ministry is weird by definition. The practice of healing, deliverance or prophecy can certainly feel weird as we do it. But I think the biggest problem among believers is not that we think supernatural ministries are too weird; it's that we try to make God seem normal. . . . No one who believes in God is entitled to reject supernatural ministries simply because they seem strange. But there's something in all of us that isn't comfortable being weird. We crave a respectable God-experience. So, we're apt to manage our emphases.[1]

> **Supernatural ministries are meant to accompany us in witness. And some encounters will demand them.**

God's power is real and available. But to embrace it we have to embrace a level of discomfort and being out of control. Supernatural ministries are meant to accompany us in witness. And some encounters will demand them. However, we have to open up our paradigms of witness, just like I did that day in Egypt, if we are going to experience them.

There Is a Cosmic Battle

After that trip in Egypt my thinking had to grow, and I searched the Scriptures to understand what I had experienced. If God is like this, why am I not experiencing this more? Am I following Scripture rightly? Many questions dashed through my mind, but over the years I was able to land on some concrete thoughts. The following are some of the key verses that have shaped the way I think about witness inside the cosmic battle that rages around this world.

"Our struggle is not against flesh and blood, but against the rulers, against the authorities, against the powers of this dark world and against the spiritual forces of evil in the heavenly realms" (Ephesians 6:12). This verse clearly helps me see that in fact a spiritual battle is happening. The rest of Ephesians 6 goes on to help us understand how to dress for this battle we are intended to fight in.

"The god of this age has blinded the minds of unbelievers, so that they cannot see the light of the gospel that displays the glory of Christ, who is the image of God" (2 Corinthians 4:4). Our friends, family members, coworkers and complete strangers we meet have minds held captive by the "god of this age." Paul, in his letters, and John, in his Gospel, make it clear that Satan is the prince of this world. Therefore, he is free to wreak havoc in this world until Jesus' second coming.

Jesus plans to do something about this, and he makes a statement about the battle of the kingdom of Satan and the kingdom of God in Mark 3:27: "In fact, no one can enter a strong man's house without first tying him up. Then he can plunder the strong man's house." Satan is the strong man, and Jesus is here to bind him. Jesus has stripped Satan of his power over all people. Satan still roams the world and has power over those not submitted to Christ. Before Jesus went to the cross, Satan had power over any person. But the kingdom of God went to war with the kingdom of Satan, and Jesus won. Satan has no power over those who choose Jesus but much power over those who do not. All people, until plundered from Satan's control, are still in his possession. Jesus has sent you, me and all of his disciples to engage in the war to take people back from the rule and power of Satan.

Clinton Arnold says,

> Having defeated Satan, Christ is able to plunder his kingdom
> through the church's evangelistic outreach. The parable of the
> binding of the strong man probably provided great encour-
> agement to the evangelistic efforts of the early church. Since
> Satan was in some sense "tied up" at the cross, the church (as
> Christ's agents) could now "carry off his possessions."[2]

We Are Called to Fight

Our mission as Christians is to go into this world, Satan's kingdom,
and plunder his goods. We are called to share the gospel and bring
people into saving knowledge of Jesus Christ. We are to rescue people
out of the grip of evil, from the path that leads to destruction, and lead
them onto the path that leads to life. That path is Jesus, and the way
people get onto this path is by believing the good news about him.

Fighting the cosmic battle with God's resources is spiritual
warfare. Making it your aim in life to plunder Satan's house and
bring people out from it and into a relationship with Jesus involves
spiritual battle. If you take seriously sharing your faith or take on
the responsibility to help people know Christ, then you are fighting
in a spiritual battle.

What is spiritual warfare? I love how Clinton Arnold puts it:
"Foundational to spiritual warfare is a belief in evil spirits and a
desire to get the upper hand on them before they get it on us."[3]
When it comes to evangelism, awareness of the spiritual realm is
critical because we are not just trying to get the upper hand on evil
for ourselves but for the people the Holy Spirit sends us to. These
people can't get the upper hand because they do not have the power
of Christ in them.

Most people are already nervous or scared to do evangelism. It
is difficult for most of us, and we feel like we need to muster up
strength and learn to share our faith. We tell ourselves we need

more willpower, discipline and drive. Or we need to love our friends more to be motivated to share our faith.

This faulty reasoning is precisely why I have written this chapter. Sharing our faith is not primarily about mustering strength but about receiving and walking in the power of the Spirit to do his works. It is understanding the battle that our world is caught in, the battle between Jesus and Satan and their two warring kingdoms.

We cannot muster enough willpower for a battle like this! When we find ourselves in situations where people need healing or deliverance, we need supernatural power from on high that

> **Sharing our faith is not primarily about mustering strength but about receiving and walking in the power of the Spirit.**

equips us to fight on behalf of people who are controlled by spirits or by sickness in their minds, bodies and souls. We need the power of the Holy Spirit so we have direction, so life comes to our words and so he can enable us to cast out demons and heal.

Key Step: Prayer and Meditation

Ask God to make you more aware of the reality of the spiritual realm. Spend some time this week meditating on the verses mentioned.

Reflection Questions

1. Describe a situation in your life (or a friend's life) that cannot be explained in a rational, logical way.

2. Describe our culture's attraction to the supernatural in movies (vampires, zombies, etc.). Given this fascination, why do we then skip over the supernatural in our daily lives?

3. What would it take for you to be more open to God using you in healings and spiritual warfare?

6

Engaging the Spiritual Battle

MANY CHRISTIANS DON'T BELIEVE in the power and dynamic nature of the spiritual realm. Some admit they don't, but many others act and live as if there is no more happening than meets the eye. Is that you?

Far too many Christians have trouble believing in the supernatural because our Western culture, as well as church theology, has all but swept spiritual warfare under the rug. We don't talk about it, we don't see it, and we don't believe in it. We are too "smart and developed" for this kind of thinking.

This saddens and baffles me. I would not have nearly the number of breakthroughs with leading seekers to Jesus if I were not pressing into the power of the Spirit in my witness. Again, the gospel saves, not miracles or deliverance. But many times we need to heal, give a word of knowledge or lead someone through deliverance before they can hear and receive the gospel of Jesus.

Are you open to that?

This may be foreign to you because apart from Pentecostal or charismatic circles, evangelical faith is primarily cognitive, lived in the head. Although the Christian faith and experience is meant to encompass the cognitive, emotional and spiritual parts of us, we Westerners primarily express our faith in cognitive ways. We explain our faith through our knowledge and understanding. Most of this can be attributed to the scientific age we live in.

You Cannot See What You Don't Believe

Though it's a generalization, it is nonetheless true that Western Christians have written off demons. The demonic doesn't make logical or scientific sense, and we cannot see them. But that is our problem: We don't believe what we cannot see. In fact, we have even stopped looking. Look at figure 6.1 and tell someone next to you what it says or write it down.

Now read it again.

Do you see the extra *the*? Most people don't. This is because your mind knows it shouldn't be there. You know it should say "I love Paris in the springtime" because that is the proper way to write and speak English. Your mind skips the extra *the*.

Fig. 6.1

We do this with all kinds of things we believe shouldn't be there. People are very good at deceiving themselves and tricking their minds to see what they want to see. Sometimes we don't see what is there even though it is present, and other times we believe we see things that are not really present.

Unfortunately, we also do this with the spiritual realm. Some people overemphasize the demonic; they see demons in every situation, even when they are not there. More often Westerners are conditioned not to see something when it is there. We skip right over the

> **Sometimes we don't see what is there even though it is present, and other times we believe we see things that are not really present.**

the in the spiritual picture; that is, we don't see the extra word—the spiritual conflict—at play.

But Paul, Jesus and the early church did not skip spiritual conflict. It was part of how they viewed the world and everyday experiences. It didn't make them feel uncomfortable to suggest that principalities and spirits may be behind things.

Philip Encounters Evil Spirits

Let's look at the beginning of Acts 8, where Philip shows up in Samaria right after the church has been scattered. This story occurs right before the Spirit sends Philip to the Ethiopian. Not only did miracles advance Philip's ministry, but he encountered evil spirits.

> Philip went down to a city in Samaria and proclaimed the Messiah there. When the crowds heard Philip and saw the signs he performed, they all paid close attention to what he said. For with shrieks, impure spirits came out of many, and many who were paralyzed or lame were healed. So there was great joy in that city. (Acts 8:5-8)

We see explicitly that Philip proclaimed Christ there, and people gave their lives to Jesus. But these people also needed spiritual victory over the satanic presence that was controlling their lives. Some of these people were controlled by, or their bodies were deformed by, demons. They needed the power of the Spirit, and that was an important part of Philip's witness that day.

Similarly, the Spirit will send you to people. Often, you'll be sent into a spiritual conflict with spiritual enemies—demons and evil spirits. It is a witness's job to confront these enemies in Jesus' name. We are sent into spiritual battle for the sake of those in bondage and in the enemy's grip.

Jesus teaches the disciples this important lesson in Mark 9:29, when they ask him why they weren't able to cast out the demon from a boy. Jesus responds, "This kind can come out only by prayer."

Some ancient biblical manuscripts say "prayer and fasting" in this verse, and we know that Jesus and the early church practiced the discipline of fasting. Some people we encounter are battling such demonic forces that we cannot simply show up and expect a breakthrough. They are battled through prayer and fasting, and we need to tap further into the supernatural power that is available to us in Jesus and through the Spirit. This is precisely what Jesus is telling his disciples.

One side of supernatural work in evangelism is miracles (hearing words of knowledge and so on); the other side is spiritual conflict. Raging around us is a spiritual battle in which Jesus and his angels are warring against Satan and his demons. We see this in Acts 8 when Philip casts out demons, but we also see this throughout the Gospels and Paul's letters. A huge part of Jesus' ministry involved releasing people from the grip of Satan. To be effective witnesses, we not only need to know how to share the gospel and how to step into miracles, but we also need to embrace the reality of spiritual battle and fight it in the Spirit. If the idea of fighting the spiritual battle on behalf of your friends isn't freaking you out, then it is leading you to ask, How am I supposed to do this, Beau? What step can I take to enter into battle to see people released from evil and into the arms of Jesus?

Preparing for Breakthrough

First, we need to learn to think accurately about our world, the theology of spiritual conflict and how to carry ourselves as a witness. Learning to think differently is not that easy. You probably have been raised with a worldview that does not include spiritual warfare. It will help to be aware that the lenses through which you've looked at the world block out the spiritual realm. The following are a few points and Scriptures you can start to meditate on and pray through.

We live amid an ongoing spiritual battle. Ephesians 6:12 says, "Our struggle is not against flesh and blood, but against the rulers, against the authorities, against the powers of this dark world and against the spiritual forces of evil in the heavenly realms." Meditate on this Scripture and ask God to make you aware of the battle around us. When entering into conversations or relationships with others, ask God to make you aware of the struggle.

Jesus won the battle and we will too. On the cross Jesus stripped Satan of his power over believers. "And having disarmed the powers and authorities, he made a public spectacle of them, triumphing over them by the cross" (Colossians 2:15). You do not need to be afraid. This is not a war between equal powers—good and evil. Jesus is victorious. He is sovereign. Even though evil runs rampant until Christ returns, his power is stronger, and we have victory in his name. Ask God to help you think victoriously and not fall into the trap of thinking that it's an equal battle.

We have no power and all the power simultaneously. As humans, in our own power, we have nothing over demons. They will kick our butts if we try to engage them or invite them in. That is what is happening to many of our friends. Many people around us dabble in the demonic and let evil forces into their lives. They find themselves powerless in certain areas of life because forces beyond their power have taken over. Think about the way you have experienced God's power to set you free of sinful patterns in your life. Some of your friends are experiencing a supernatural power who is controlling them and taking them deeper into sin and darkness. They need you to show up with a greater power and to know how to help free them. Beforehand, you need to pray for them to be released so when you show up they have clarity to hear and respond to the gospel. You have all the power in Christ Jesus, in fact the same power that raised him from the dead (Ephesians 1:18-20).

We don't need to chase demons, but they are there. I don't suggest that you try to find demons in every encounter you have. Don't do that. It is weird and not helpful. But you do need to be aware.

Every time you are sent into an encounter, ask God what he is doing in this situation. Also ask him to reveal any interference or dark force that is with the person you have met. There may not be anything, and that is fine. Continue on. Be aware, though, that there very well could be something. "Be sober, be vigilant; because your adversary the devil, as a roaring lion, walketh about, seeking whom he may devour" (1 Peter 5:8 KJV).

Fast and pray. When I get stuck in my witness and I am not experiencing a breakthrough with a person, I step back and spend some time fasting and praying (Mark 9:29).[1] I recently saw a man come to faith after fasting for him only one day. This guy started coming to our ministry, and he was genuinely curious about finding a relationship with God. He had never stepped into a relationship with Christ, and he was living wildly at the time. We had great conversation and studied Scripture, but there was just no breakthrough. There was some kind of interference. Nothing was connecting. He wasn't disagreeing or arguing with us. It felt like I was on a phone call with him and there was static on the line. He just couldn't hear me or hear God. Whenever I have situations like this, I take it as a sign that demonic forces are interfering. So I step back, fast and pray and ask God to break through in the spiritual realm. I need more power from God.

Fasting allows me to enter into a posture that says, "God, I need more than I can give." Fasting from food is the best way to feel totally weak and helpless. It's the best way to help us enter into urgent prayer for people and call on God, who has all the power. It reminds me that I cannot do anything without God. Even more, Jesus says that some things can only come out through prayer, so I want to take that seriously and press in.

In this particular situation I asked a few friends to fast and pray with me for one day before I met again with the guy. I knew he was close to accepting Christ, but we needed to clear some of the spiritual funk out of the air. The next day when I went to meet with him, something was different. The atmosphere was changed, and so was his countenance. I walked him through the story of the woman at the well in John 4, and we had a direct conversation about Jesus wanting to exchange his source of life and replace it with himself. Jesus offers him living water, but he must drop his "bucket" and what he is filling his life with. He was curious and wanted the living water Jesus offered. I was able to explain to him the cross, the free gift of salvation and how relationship with Jesus works. He accepted Christ on the spot, and we prayed together in joy. He said to me, "I have never heard the cross explained that way before. It makes so much sense that Jesus would die for our sins, bury them and then rise again to give us new life."

I laughed because I knew he had heard that before. However, he had spiritual interference and couldn't perceive the message. As we continue to meet and learn to follow Jesus, my friends and I are still fasting and praying for his discipleship.

Asking for Breakthrough

You need another tool in your spiritual tool belt for spiritual warfare. Healing prayer is the best all-around tool you can use to fight the deeper spiritual battle for your friends. I suggest healing prayer because I believe it is the most relational and healthy way for the average person to start out in spiritual battle. I like it because you can learn with others as you help them pray for people and for you. You will learn to hear from God, receive Scriptures, words of knowledge and images from him that will speak deeply into people's lives.

Some of my most powerful times of ministry have come from doing healing prayer with others.

Some of my most powerful times of ministry have come from doing healing prayer with others.

During a worship service I was leading, a powerful time of healing prayer led to a conversion. A woman who was not following Jesus was off to the side praying with a friend, and Jesus spoke powerfully to her. As the seeking woman prayed, a painful childhood memory came to her. In that memory Jesus revealed himself to her, and she heard him speak to her for the first time. He told her that she could trust him and he would heal her. She heard God so clearly that she committed her life to Christ right there. It was so powerful for her that at the end of the service she stood before the whole group and testified that she had accepted Christ.

Healing prayer unlocks spiritual strongholds in people's lives. Sometimes the demonic forces don't manifest themselves because the power of Jesus quietly drives them away. The person feels free, peaceful or clearheaded, and that is a sign that the darkness is gone. But at other times healing prayer can drive things to the surface in more dramatic ways. But we have the power in Christ to bind these spirits and send them packing.

Again, when I get stuck in my witness, I love to offer to pray with people who are seeking Jesus. Just the other day I offered to pray for a neighbor who confessed to me some serious pain in his life. He was open to it—as weird as it was to ask him to pray with me. I am now preparing to get together with him and pray about his painful experience. I am hopeful Jesus will reveal himself in prayer to my neighbor, and he will begin to follow Jesus.

Praying for people is a great way to do evangelism. As you grow deeper in relationship with a person who doesn't know Jesus, try praying for the person and asking him or her to wait on God with you for a word that speaks into their life. Many people that aren't ready to have a conversation about Jesus will let you pray for them if you ask. They may need something broken off spiritually before they are able to say yes to Jesus.[2]

While healing prayer does not replace counseling or a significant change in the person's heart or mind, sometimes deeper spiritual strongholds need to be broken so the person can truly get healthy or come to the Lord.

Key Step: Fast and Pray

Go back to chapter one where you wrote down the five names of people who are waiting for a witness. Pick a day next week to fast from food for them if you can. If you can't do a whole day, then pick a meal. If you can't fast from food, then pick something you normally do on that day and leave it out (like television, social media or eating meat). But fast from food if you can. During your mealtimes, pray instead of eating. Ask God to break through to your friends and release them from Satan's grip (2 Corinthians 4:4). Pray for opportunities to share your faith in the coming week when your friends are more open.

Reflection Questions

1. Which of the Scriptures shared in this chapter strikes you the most?

2. Think of a person in your life who is not open to God. Start praying for God to show that person his supernatural power.

A WITNESS AT WORK

Down the Sports Road

**Brock Huard, former NFL quarterback,
and current college football analyst for ESPN
and radio host for ESPN Seattle**

"The media world, like the locker rooms I once inhabited, is an incredible mission field," says Brock Huard.

Brock spent six years in the NFL. His big brother, Damon, spent twelve years in the NFL, and his little brother, Luke, is an NCAA Division 1 coach. They are a football family, and Brock has had the game in his life since he was born. Football has paved the way for many opportunities, one of which is the opportunity to share Christ with many the church doesn't reach.

"Much like my teammates of old, people are thirsting for authentic and genuine leaders," Brock says. While he had plenty of spiritual opportunities during his playing years, he now finds himself in a totally different mission field—the broadcasting world. Weekly I hear Brock talking about Christ on air in the most appropriate ways he can, and I know he is having conversations behind the scenes. He is a tremendous man of influence, and the key question he is asking every day is how to use that for Jesus.

"There was nothing quite like calling a play in a huddle and having everyone looking to your guidance. And when I understand my Savior wants me to call his plays—everyday, in every environment he leads me in—I start to understand the call to not score touchdowns, but save lives." That is Brock's ultimate call, and he finds his reward not in the worship of fans but in the exciting arena of angels, saints and the kingdom of God.

How to Hear God's Voice in Witness

I WAS HAVING A BURRITO with a guy named Sam when, right in the middle of our conversation, I sensed God saying, "Ask him if he struggles with his sexuality." It caught me off-guard because we were not talking about relationships, dating or sex.

Adding further to my internal tension was that Sam didn't come across in any way as someone who would struggle in this area. I had never suspected anything and was almost certain that none of the people in our ministry did either. This word from God came out of left field. It was the first time we had ever met for a one-on-one meeting, so I didn't have a lot of trust built with him. If I were to ask Sam this question, it could be totally offensive, to say the least. It seemed to be a huge risk.

But the bigger questions in my heart were: Was God really speaking to me? Did I believe I had heard the voice of God? Would God even say something like that?

It is one thing to believe God is speaking and then obey what he's said when it seems easy and clear. It's easy to believe and obey when there's no risk. But what about when the costs are high? When relationships, credibility, reputation or even my life is on the line?

This is when it is important to know what the voice of God sounds like and to be confident that the Spirit speaks. God is forging ways to open conversations and break into people's lives. One of the primary ways God does that is by giving certain directions, words, Scriptures and images to his witnesses.

Pause now and consider: Do you believe God speaks to you? Do you believe God speaks in the midst of your daily life, and even in the middle of a conversation? Do you believe God speaks things that might make you uncomfortable?

You Are Meant to Hear God's Voice

You are meant to hear God's voice, and you are meant to follow it. The Scriptures are loaded with examples of God speaking to his people, and the same is true for us today—especially when it comes to witness. Jesus teaches in Luke 15:1-7 that God is like a good shepherd who pursues every lost sheep, whom he is passionate about finding and training to hear his voice. In fact, Jesus uses his disciples to find these sheep, as we see more clearly later in the book of Acts. How does he send his disciples? By speaking to and calling them to follow him and witness to his name.

Hearing God's voice is a key trait that marks all of Jesus' disciples in the book of Acts (and throughout the New Testament, for that matter). They hear the voice of our Lord loud and clear, and they follow,

> **You are meant to hear God's voice, and you are meant to follow it.**

even to death. The disciples are led by the voice of God, and they seemingly don't take a step without his prompting. As you read the pages of the New Testament, you see Spirit-dependent believers. They seem to believe unequivocally that the Holy Spirit speaks, and we see that no more clearly than through their bold acts of faith.

Consequently, New Testament believers' lives are adventurous, thrilling, frightening and full of persecution. They are also marked by joy and purpose. They witness firsthand as families turn to Jesus, paralyzed people stand up, the sight of the blind is restored and the dead are resurrected. They also get imprisoned, beaten and even killed. All this happens because they follow the voice of Jesus.

Following God's voice is not safe, but it is full of life. Following Jesus' voice every step of the way is how life is meant to be. We are created to hear him, to be led by him, to follow him, to be released by him.

Following God's voice is not safe, but it is full of life.

To become a witness who regularly sees people come to faith, you will have to learn to hear Jesus' voice and follow it. There are encounters waiting to happen that you won't find without him leading you. Jesus has faith encounters set up for people far away from him, but they need a witness. They need someone to tell them about Jesus. As Paul says,

> How, then, can they call on the one they have not believed in? And how can they believe in the one of whom they have not heard? And how can they hear without someone preaching to them? And how can anyone preach unless they are sent? As it is written: "How beautiful are the feet of those who bring good news!" (Romans 10:14-15)

Before people can believe, they must hear. Before they hear, they must have someone preach to them. Before someone can preach, he or she must be sent. And before the witness is sent, he or she must hear the voice of God calling to go.

God is actively looking for witnesses to send into the harvest, and he is speaking all the time. Do you believe God is speaking? Can you hear him? Do you hear him? Do you believe he wants to speak to you about your family, your neighborhood, your school, your work and even the person you will have lunch with tomorrow?

Two Objections

Many believers challenge the notion that God actively speaks to us today. One common objection is, God has already spoken in the canonized Scriptures, so I follow that. What do you mean God wants to speak to me personally? Another objection I hear frequently is, I am not one of those people who hear from God. I cannot even tell you the last time I heard from him, if ever. That is for those prayer people who are more spiritually connected. I just do my best to follow what the Bible says and do good in the world. Sound familiar? I bet you have heard people talk like this. Maybe you have said something similar yourself. So let me push back on these objections a bit.

First, the idea that God has already spoken and Scripture is our guide is 100 percent true. Nothing we hear from God in our day should ever contradict his Word. But the idea that God doesn't continually speak to us because he has already spoken is not necessarily true. These aren't mutually exclusive.

Follow my reasoning. God gave the clear mandate in Scripture that we are to witness to the ends of the world.

Then Jesus came to them and said, "All authority in heaven and on earth has been given to me. Therefore go and make disciples of all nations, baptizing them in the name of the Father and of the Son and of the Holy Spirit, and teaching them to obey everything I have commanded you. And surely I am with you always, to the very end of the age." (Matthew 28:18-20)

You will receive power when the Holy Spirit comes on you; and you will be my witnesses in Jerusalem, and in all Judea and Samaria, and to the ends of the earth. (Acts 1:8)

The scriptural mandate to be witnesses and make disciples of all nations for the rest of time is God's *general revelation*. He has spoken, and every Christian is called to actively look for people to share Jesus with. To understand our call to "go" generally, we do not need another word spoken—God has made it clear.

But God also intends to speak to you every day about the specifics inside this general mission.

I have said these things to you while I am still with you. But
the Advocate, the Holy Spirit, whom the Father will send in
my name, will teach you everything, and remind you of all
that I have said to you. (John 14:25-26 NRSV)

Whenever you are arrested and brought to trial, do not
worry beforehand about what to say. Just say whatever is
given you at the time, for it is not you speaking, but the Holy
Spirit. (Mark 13:11)

Let's say you have a boss who says, "Go to Boston and pick up
materials." It is not good enough to simply know you are supposed
to go there. You need to know exactly what materials he wants,
where to pick them up and who to get them from. And you may
need course corrections along the way. To say it is enough that God
has already spoken in Scripture is like saying I know my work as-
signment and won't need to ask my boss clarifying questions or
check in with him about how it's going.

Scripture is essential, of course, and nothing we hear further in
the process should contradict the Word. But we need to ask God
for updates. Once God has told me to do something, I am constantly checking with him about the process and asking him for
new images or words to direct me or encourage me. Then I check
them against Scripture. If I can't find Scripture to back up what I
am hearing and sensing, I let the word pass as not from God.

For example, when I am meeting with someone, I may take a
minute to pray for, or even with, the person before the meeting. I
regularly ask God for an image or a word, and he often gives me
one. The other day I was praying for someone and God gave me an
image of roots. Later, this person told me he had been feeling lost
in life, so I shared with him the roots image and encouraged him
that God may want to "ground" him further. I asked the person if
that resonated. He said it totally resonated, and then I began to
share John 15 with him, that we are to abide in Christ. We connect

ourselves to Christ, and he is where we find nourishment and grounding. This image is very scriptural, and God gave it to me to encourage this person to go deeper in his Word. (When I took a minute and thought about why I got the image of roots and how that could connect with Scripture and God's character, he put in my mind John 15.)

Many times when I am praying for someone or for some direction, I get images or words that make no sense. I write them down, but if I can't easily connect it to Scripture or it doesn't resonate with the person when I share, then I let it go as not from God. I don't dwell on it and move on.

My call to witness is *general*—every day I am looking for opportunities because that is Jesus' mandate. But I want to know God and his plans more intimately. I want him to give me Scriptures to share, images to help me pray and steps to follow. Jesus shows us in Scripture that he intends to speak to and direct us through the Holy Spirit. I press into this every day. I want God to speak to me and lead me into the kind of encounters I see in the New Testament. Jesus said we would do greater works than he did. How can I do these if I am not listening to and following his voice?

I realize this may seem like I am asking you to follow a micromanaging God. But I do not see it like that. I see God as a great partner in witness. Think about the smartest finance person you know: If you

> **Jesus said we would do greater works than he did. How can I do these if I am not listening to and following his voice?**

could seek financial guidance from this person at any moment, wouldn't you? If you were in an important meeting or had to make a financial decision and were confused, wouldn't you want to call this person and ask what to do? That is not micromanaging for two reasons. First, you are asking for this person's opinion. Second, this person would be releasing you into more creativity and possibilities because he or she can see how your money could go further than you can. God is the same. He knows people best. He knows our steps before we take them. Why not check in with him regularly about what to do next and how to invest your time and words?

The second common objection is that some (many?) people don't hear from God—that is not how it works for them. But John 10 and many Scriptures in Acts and the epistles seem to say that hearing from God isn't for some believers and not for others. It is central to a relationship with Christ. He lives inside us through the Holy Spirit.

> Given our basic nature, we live—really live—only through God's regular speaking in our souls and thus "by every word that comes from the mouth of God." . . .
>
> We might well ask, "How could there be a personal relationship, a personal walk with God—or with anyone else—*without* individualized communication?"[1]

A major reason many people do not see others around them come to faith is that they are not regularly asking God for directions. Many of my evangelistic encounters are successful not because I am a gifted evangelist but because I asked God to show me what he was doing in that situation. People—perhaps you—have to stop making the excuse that they don't hear God that way. It is time to learn how. People are waiting for you to show up!

> **A major reason many people do not see others around them come to faith is that they are not regularly asking God for directions.**

Do You Question Your Sexuality?

In my heart I was certain God had just given me a word of knowledge, but that didn't stop me from sweating. I knew God was asking me to bring up Sam's sexuality, not to condemn him but to love him and show him that God knows even his inward thoughts. Psalm 139 came to mind, and especially the verse about how God perceives our "going out and lying down." He knows us. This was an opportunity to show this young man that God was in his corner and knew what was happening deep inside him.

But what if I was wrong? What if I heard God incorrectly? What if the guy freaked out? I couldn't worry about that any longer. Instead, I was now concerned that I would miss the moment or deliver the word poorly.

A few moments later into our conversation, I said in the gentlest voice possible, "Sam, I know this is a weird question, but do you struggle with your sexuality?" With eyes widening, Sam looked me in the face, then glanced down and to the left. I will never forget the moment. In an embarrassed and shamed voice he responded, "How did you know? I never told anyone that before. Actually, I am not even sure if I do. I am confused. I wanted to talk to someone but didn't even know how."

Totally relieved that I didn't blow it, I jumped right in and explained, "God revealed that to me, and he revealed it not to shame you but to bring healing and clarity to you. God sees you, Sam. He is in this with you."

Sam felt loved in that moment, and we continued talking about it a few times after that day. I was called to ministry in Los Angeles a year later, but I stay in touch with Sam. He trusts me. He is still confused and in a season of avoiding the pain of his struggle. He had some hard things happen growing up and doesn't want to go there at the moment.

God spoke that day to Sam, and I heard it. I believed it was God and acted on that belief. It took a word of knowledge to get to the deepest parts of him. He wasn't going to offer up that information, even though he wanted to be free from the secret. God needed to speak, God wanted to speak, and God did speak. This breakthrough blessed Sam and made him feel loved and safe.

I want to see this kind of breakthrough frequently. I want the kind of life where the voice of God is heard regularly and clearly. It is a Spirit-led life full of excitement. I want to be on adventure with God, and I want him to use me in bold, daring and costly ways that will facilitate his love pouring into others' lives in fresh and powerful ways. Just like it happened for Sam that sunny afternoon.

Don't you want that kind of life too? One way you are going to get that life is to let the Spirit continually speak to you about witness. It takes some guts to ask God to speak to you and actively wait on his voice. But his direct leading is absolutely necessary in order to witness the kind of powerful encounters that line the pages of the New Testament.

I say you need a gut check. Do you have the stomach to engage God this way?

"My sheep listen to my voice; I know them, and they follow me" (John 10:27).

How to Hear God and Follow His Promptings

If we are going to follow the Spirit into witness, we have to know how to discern his voice and follow his lead. Those looking for more general guidance on discerning God's voice or learning how to hear from him should check appendix one for five clear guidelines. (In a nutshell, these are [1] checking what you hear against Scripture, [2] prayer, [3] the fruit, [4] community and [5] faith.)

But here I want to focus on what it means to hear God's voice on the move. How do we know if God is speaking when we are pounding the pavement, so to speak? How do we discern his voice and act on it—especially when it is awkward or even dicey? What are promptings, and how do we get them and move on them?

1. Trust that God is speaking and wants to speak. First, it is important to realize that God is speaking to us and his desire is for us to hear him and converse with him. God has been speaking to his people since creation, and nothing in Scripture says he has stopped. God does not want it to be difficult to hear his voice. Choosing to believe this makes all the difference. He wants to converse with us, especially about witness and helping others know him. We have to take this mindset with us to the office, to the park, while we're working out at the gym and while on campus. God will whisper to us about what he is doing with people around us, and we need to be able to hear him.

Because some of us do not hear God often (or not at all), it may be hard to trust that God speaks today. It's easy to write off the notion that God speaks to us, because if he did, it would be easier to decipher. Dallas Willard couldn't disagree more:

> We may mistakenly think that if *God* spoke to us we would automatically know who is speaking, without having to learn, but that is simply a mistake—and one of the most harmful mistakes for those trying to hear God's voice. It leaves us totally at the mercy of any stray ideas we have picked up about what God's speaking is like.[2]

Learning to hear from God can be difficult. It takes time to discern a person's voice. But after some time listening to the person and interacting with him or her, we start to pick it out of the crowd of other voices. Because something takes practice doesn't mean it isn't essential to our being.

2. Pay attention to how you feel. When I am in a conversation with someone, or when I'm out and about, I often take a moment to ask myself, *How am I feeling?* I want to be aware of any joy or tension present. One of my friends feels a strong sense of compassion for a person when he is about to be prompted by God. I tend to feel a burden or weight in moments before a prompting.

Jesus felt similar things. "When he saw the crowds, he had compassion on them, because they were harassed and helpless, like sheep without a shepherd" (Matthew 9:36). The compassion Jesus had was not some heart feeling. It was a deep, gut-wrenching pain. He was deeply bothered by what he saw, and it prompted him to act. Right after this he sent his disciples out. No coincidence, I'm sure.

Sure, this is not the audible voice of God, but sometimes a deep compassion or burden for something can be a clear sign that God is prompting us to act in a particular situation. This is one way he speaks to us.

We are body, mind and soul. Our bodies can tell us how our soul is doing. Do I bank everything on how I am feeling? Of course not! But not paying attention to our whole person is to ignore part of how God may be speaking. Over my years of following Jesus, I have learned that he speaks to me through that "heaviness," and I have learned to pay attention to it. I have learned through trial and error that when I feel that in my body, God is about to speak or is speaking—I then pay extra attention in that moment.

Our bodies can tell us how our soul is doing.

3. Listen for the inner voice that is God. When I feel the burden or itch in my soul that must be scratched, and when my friend feels compassion, we stop and ask God, "What do you want me to say?" or "What do you want me to know or do?" With one ear listening to the person and the other to God, we take a minute to wait for the voice of God deep within us—the Holy Spirit who is alive and active.

This is what happened with my downstairs neighbor, and with Sam over a burrito. Both times I felt that something needed to happen. With my neighbor, after interacting with the missionaries, I felt a burden: *This is not right; she needs to know the truth about God.* Then God spoke to me: "Go talk to her." It was as if I was talking to myself. That's how clear it was. With Sam, it was an upsurge of curiosity in my soul and a sense from God that there was more below the surface. So I asked God, "What is here that I can't see but you want to reveal?" Then I suddenly had the idea, *Ask him about his sexuality.* That was so unexpected that I decided it was not my own idea but God speaking to me. So I stepped out in trust, and God was in fact speaking. "To one there is given through the Spirit a message of wisdom, to another a message of knowledge by means of the same Spirit" (1 Corinthians 12:8). Or as G. Campbell Morgan said,

> The doctrine of the inner light is not sufficiently taught. To the individual believer, who is, by the very fact of relationship to Christ, indwelt by the Holy Spirit of God, there is granted the direct impression of the Spirit of God on the spirit of man, imparting the knowledge of His Will in matters of the smallest and greatest importance. This has to be sought and waited for.[3]

4. Take risks and learn to trust. In these moments when God speaks from deep within, we have the option to ignore it and move forward, or to take a risk and learn to trust it. Only through practice have I learned to hone my ability to understand the voice of God more clearly. Many times I have had a sense about someone and stepped out, and I was wrong. Nothing was there. So I paid the awkward bill and politely said, "Sorry about that; it must be me then."

But many times I have stepped out and have been right in step with God's Spirit. Each time I have missed or hit it right on, it has taught me more clearly what God's voice sounds like and how to follow the promptings I get while on the move. Many times we ignore these promptings because they seem too simple or too much like our own voice. But let me assure you again, God wants to speak to us, and he does. It *will* sound familiar, and often it *will* be simple. As you and I both know, the simplest direction can sometimes be the hardest to follow!

In John 2, Jesus gave a clear direction to the servants, but it was still hard to follow and very risky. "Jesus said to the servants, 'Fill the jars with water'; so they filled them to the brim. Then he told them, 'Now draw some out and take it to the master of the banquet'" (John 2:7-8).

5. Is this in line with Scripture and God's character? I cannot overemphasize the importance of knowing Scripture and reading it. This is how we learn the character of God and his voice. It is how I filter every interaction I have with him or other people. For example, when I sense God is asking me to say something to someone, I filter what I think I need to say with what I know about Scripture and God's character. Would he say this kind of thing to a person? Has he said this to someone in the Scriptures? I have story after story of Jesus in mind, and I am able to quickly discern if this is the voice of God, my own or the enemy's. God's voice is inviting. It can be correcting, but it is not condemning or shaming.

When I had the idea to ask Sam about his sexuality, I had many questions. *Would God ask this?* In John 4, Jesus presses into the sexual and romantic life of the woman at the well.

He told her, "Go, call your husband and come back."

"I have no husband," she replied.

Jesus said to her, "You are right when you say you have no husband. The fact is, you have had five husbands, and the man you now have is not your husband. What you have just said is quite true." (John 4:16-18)

Furthermore, I know from Scripture that Jesus put himself in many risky situations by talking with strangers. Paul and the other disciples and apostles did too. Because of that, I never want to shut down what I feel is a prompting from God because it is strange or unfamiliar. The awkwardness God is asking you and me to step into pales in comparison to the risky situations Jesus and his disciples entered. Getting an awkward stare from a roommate or coworker isn't so bad when we contrast it with Jesus potentially getting stoned and eventually giving his life for our salvation. Read through the New Testament again asking one question: What kinds of strange things does Jesus or the Holy Spirit ask his followers to do? You will find things that will make your risks pale in comparison.

Key Step: Take Baby Steps

The best thing you can do to start learning to hear God's voice is to try. The Holy Spirit lives inside you and intends to speak to you. Have fun with it.

Before you go outside. Get quiet and start paying attention to what the Spirit is saying to you. Pay attention to Scripture, images, senses and people that come to mind. Pay attention to how you feel.

One of the biggest reasons we don't hear God is that we don't ask specific questions. God may say something, but often my mind is so distracted and jumping all over the place that I can't focus on his voice. I try to quiet myself but immediately start thinking of all the things I need to do. But when I ask a specific question, I often sense an immediate response. You can ask general questions, like, "Lord, what do you want to say to me right now?" or "Do you have a direction for me today?" You can also ask more specific questions, like, "This person is irritating me. What should I do?" Try it!

Often the answer will come in a quiet and sometimes even partial way. I may get the beginning of a thought or sentence or picture, but as I accept that and go with it, God fills it out more and more. It feels like it takes an initial step of faith to lean toward the Spirit and begin listening to that word, and then I become receptive enough to hear the rest of it.

Don't be discouraged if you have to try this several times before you sense God speaking to you. Every intimate relationship we have requires time, and our relationship with God is no different. However, God is eager to communicate with us, and I am sure that with persistence you will learn to discern the Spirit's voice.

Remember, discerning the Spirit's voice is tied with knowing Scripture. So as you get images or words to the questions you are asking, always take those and anchor them with a Scripture. I find that when I anchor an image or word in Scripture, the Scripture takes me much deeper into understanding what God is saying and wants me to do.

I like to write in a journal what I sense from God. Then, I ask him questions about it. It's like having a conversation. I write everything down line by line as I pray, which I often look at later. I sometimes show it to my group of friends, bringing it into community, if I am worried I may be off. I ask them to help me find Scriptures to go with what I am sensing from God.

When you are out and about. When you are in the presence of others, ask the Holy Spirit questions. As you are in conversation or at a break, ask God specific questions about the person or environment. He will speak to you and let you in on what he is doing in these situations.

Don't worry if you get it wrong or are confused at first. Just give it a try! God will speak to you.

Reflection Questions

1. When you think about hearing from God, what concerns arise?

2. How do you feel when you try to hear from God but don't hear anything?

3. Write down one general question and one or two specific questions you have for God right now. Now take a minute to ask God and write down anything you hear or sense in your imagination.

4. Next week, lean into one of the five guidelines for hearing promptings.

A WITNESS AT WORK

Down the Mom Road

Kelly Curran, a wife and mother of three

"As a wife and mother," Kelly Curran tells me, "I'm often immersed in the needs of my family. Yet heavy on my heart is the need to tell loved ones about how Jesus rescued me from myself. I long for the people in my life to experience that same deliverance."

Kelly's primary mission field is her family and raising three kids. But she is constantly pursuing and cultivating relationships with other moms, neighbors and service providers. As we have talked, I am impressed by her willingness to be honest about her struggles and to let others into her stories of transformation. She allows those she is witnessing to into these areas so they can see how she is changing—and who is responsible for that change.

Beyond caring for her family and neighbors, Kelly has led the way in a summer outreach on her street. Her family hosted a block party for seventy neighbors. They went to fifty households and delivered invitations. Even the kids helped, and they loved it! With this block party Kelly hoped to build deeper relationships and to understand better how to care for people in the neighborhood. She is building trust so more of those authentic conversations she loves to get in could happen in the future.

"Their eternal salvation is on the line," Kelly says. "Risking rejection or ridicule is worth it."

Interlude

A Powerful Official

AMARE, A FINANCIAL OFFICER from a North African embassy, was staying in Washington, DC, for a few weeks. During his weekends off, Amare took walks in the neighborhood near his hotel. On Sundays he would pause a few minutes to listen to the music coming from inside a church he passed on his route. Finally, on his third and final weekend in DC, he decided to visit the church to see what the music was about.

He arrived ten minutes early, nervous about being among so many strangers, not to mention not knowing how church services worked in the United States. Amare believed there was a God, but he had never gone further than attending a service or two back home.

He made his way into a pew and smiled hesitantly at the older couple on his right. He noticed they snuck a few glances at him after he sat down. So did nearly everyone in the rows around him. He sat silently, waiting for the service to start, weighing whether he should stay or go. But Amare knew why he had come. Besides, a woman with two small children sat down on his left, so he couldn't make an easy exit anymore.

A few songs were sung. Amare hummed along as best he could. When the preacher started reading the Scripture, something gripped his heart. *Who was this man the preacher was reading about? Like a sheep? Like a lamb?* The description was fascinating. Amare noticed everyone else had books they were using to follow along. He saw one just like it in the back of the pew in front of him. He pulled it into his lap and then realized he had no clue what page they were on. He tried to follow along with the preacher for the rest of the service.

Immediately after the last song ended, Amare turned to the woman with two children and asked sheepishly, "What was that the preacher was reading?"

The woman motioned for the book in his hands. She flipped through it and found the page she was looking for. "That was Isaiah 53:7-8," she said. "That is an interesting passage, isn't it? You can take this Bible with you, if you don't have one. Our church gives them away for free." She turned to the younger of her children, who was tugging at her shirt.

Amare bent the corner of the page and closed the book, said a hurried thank-you and made his way back to the hotel to collect his luggage.

In the cab on the way to the airport, he couldn't stop thinking about that Scripture. He was fascinated by the person it was talking about.

After checking in and going through security, Amare pulled the book out of his briefcase and opened to the dog-eared page:

He was oppressed and afflicted,
>   yet he did not open his mouth;
he was led like a lamb to the slaughter,
>   and as a sheep before its shearers is silent,
>   so he did not open his mouth.
By oppression and judgment he was taken away.
>   Yet who of his generation protested?
For he was cut off from the land of the living;
>   for the transgression of my people he was punished.

He felt a firm tap on his shoulder.

"Excuse me," said a young man with a backpack covered in patches from all over the world. "I couldn't help but overhear you. Do you understand what you're reading?"

Amare hadn't realized he had been reading aloud. For that matter, he hadn't noticed that someone sat next to him.

"No, I don't," Amare answered. "I am trying to figure it out, but not doing so well."

"Well, if you don't mind," the young man said, "I would love to explain it to you. I'm Phil." He held out his hand.

"I'm Amare." They shook hands.

Amare was ecstatic. He couldn't believe a stranger in the airport could actually help him.

He eagerly handed Phil the book. Phil told him more about that Scripture and ended up flipping further into the book and telling Amare about someone named Jesus.

Amare instantly fell in love with this Jesus. This was the God he had been looking for but never understood. His heart was so happy he could hardly contain himself. He wanted to start singing one of the songs from the church service again.

He asked Phil what he should do now that he knew about Jesus. Phil explained how he could devote his life to Jesus from that point forward.

"Do you want to become a follower of Jesus today?" Phil asked.

"Most definitely. Yes," Amare said, and Phil showed him how to pray.

As Amare opened his eyes and sat back with a happy sigh, he heard over the intercom, "Attention, passengers, we will begin pre-boarding our business class in five minutes."

It was time to go home, but he felt like he was already there.

8

God's Role

Send and Set Up

DECEMBER 23, 2007. I was at a Seattle Seahawks game with my nephew on that rainy Sunday afternoon. Most of my family was in town for Christmas and looking forward to celebrating together. On the way back to my parents' house, I got an urgent call from my wife alerting me that something had gone wrong in a family relationship. I can't get into the details, but do know it was a horrific three days.

No one else in my family was a Christian except my younger sister, and it couldn't have been more apparent than at that time. There was no talk of a bigger picture, or a greater plan, or how God might have been in this situation. All our conversations felt like it was up to us or bust.

I decided to pray and ask God for clarity on the situation. He showed me a picture of a wall, which caught me off guard, so I asked God about the meaning. I felt like the Lord gave me this interpretation of the wall:

"Your family can't see past five feet. It is as if there is a wall in front of their faces, and they can't see what I am doing past the wall. There is no bigger perspective here. Beau, I want you to keep praying for perspective and that they would see me. Oh, and I want you to extend your trip and stay longer."

I was scheduled to leave Seattle the day after Christmas. I didn't get the full picture of what God was doing right then, but I decided to obey the directions that were clear, to stay and be present. I extended my trip, put my wife on a plane home, and waited for what was next.

I kept praying into the wall image, asking God to break through: "Please, God, help my family know who you are, so they can have your perspective in this season."

The breakthrough came the next night, December 27. My mom and stepdad were at a holiday party. Yoshiko, my sister-in-law, who was directly affected by some of this news, was still in Seattle too—with four-month-old twins, no less. I decided to stay home with her and help her with whatever she needed. I didn't know her very well; we hadn't ever talked much because she lived in Idaho and I lived in California. Plus her English was not very good.

But God was up to something that night. I could sense it. I soon felt him nudge me to strike up a conversation with her about him. She was in the living room reading, and I was in the kitchen watching TV. The twins were asleep, so I decided to walk into the living room and ask her a simple question.

"Did you know that I am a Christian?"

"Yes," she responded, "I did."

"Do you know what that means?" I asked.

"No, I don't," she replied. "Not really."

I asked her if I could tell her what I believe about Jesus but that I wanted to hear what she already believed first. You won't believe what Yoshiko said next.

She told me that she believed God lived in the *wall*. She said when she gets scared or anxious, she prays to the corners of the wall and asks God to help her. I still had no idea why she believed God lived in the wall, but the wall I'd seen suddenly made sense . . . as crazy is it was.

I explained the message of Jesus, trying my best to relate it to her current circumstances. I talked about Jesus' death and resurrection, and how if Jesus could rise from the dead, he can help her rise above her problems too. I told her God had a bigger perspective on what our family was enduring, and that she would need to invite Jesus into her life so she could hear from him and see what he saw. I asked her if she wanted to know this God. She said yes. We prayed right there for Jesus to come into her life. After many tears, we called it a night.

I wasn't sure how much she really took in; the language and cultural barriers made it hard to be sure whether she was really saying yes to God or simply to make me feel good. I felt confident in my obedience, however, and that was all I could count on.

But over the next month God was working behind the scenes. I found out that the next month my younger sister, Gina, returned to Seattle for a few days and began to talk with Yoshiko about getting a Japanese Bible and going to a Japanese church. That conversation then prompted Yoshiko to reach out to one of her only friends in town who could speak both Japanese and English, and the woman happened to be a Japanese evangelist! Sanae is her name, and she quickly connected Yoshiko to a Japanese Bible and got her plugged into the church. When I returned to the Northwest in February, I was able to meet Sanae as well and we had a great conversation with Yoshiko about what it means to follow Jesus.

Later that summer I watched her get baptized. She now hosts a Bible study in her house. God truly pursued and rescued her in that dark time.

God Sets "It" Up

Clearly, God set up my encounter with Yoshiko. He positioned me to be in Seattle, he set up our time to talk, he opened her heart to the gospel, and Gina was there to follow up and to explain the importance of a Bible and a church, and then Sanae was there to connect her to that church and baptism. I love this story because it shows that God is the current pulling people together and toward himself. We just need to jump in and play our part—in this case it was a team effort between me, Gina and Sanae, again, a beautiful picture of a witnessing community.

Recently Yoshiko emailed me after hearing me talk about her in a sermon, and she shared this with me:

> I too remember clearly that night I first met Jesus. I knew it might be very awkward for you to start talking about Jesus to someone who doesn't speak English well. But believe it or not, that night I anticipated and wanted to here [sic] about God from you. I had known you for 6 years at that time, and I was always curious to know how you became Christian and why you were so different compared to before you were Christian. I knew that you knew something very important that I never had known. If you wouldn't have taken the risk to talk about Jesus that night, I wouldn't have believed in him and accept [sic] him into my life. You were my first witness of the Lord. It was perfect timing, and I know it wasn't a co-incident [sic]. God had and has a very special plan for me. Even though I didn't understand English very well, I did totally understand what you told me. It was so amazing that the holy sprit helped me.
>
> I love that you told me "you don't need to find a corner of the wall anymore because God is all around you, he is always with you." Did you know how I started praying to the wall? Because of Shinto ("the way of the gods," Japans [sic] major religion to this day). I got a wooden amulet when I was 18 years old. I had to put it on a corner of the wall and pray every single day until I became 19 years old. (19 is a unlucky number) That's why I start praying to the wall. I didn't know that I was worshiping an idol. And I'm so glad that God showed you the wall imagine [sic] that time you were praying.

I'd like to say thank you for stepping out of your comfort zone and for your faithfulness. I couldn't have survived without Jesus these last 7 years.

So often we think that in order for evangelism to happen, it is up to us. We feel like we have to muster up the strength and courage, get the right things to say and then go. We act as if there is no momentum and we have to be the catalyst to get it all started. But what I want to help you see is that the Holy Spirit plays a major role in setting up encounters—both sending us as witnesses and initiating with seekers.

We see this no more clearly than with Philip and the Ethiopian in Acts 8. This story illustrates the Spirit's initiation and orchestration of someone's conversion

> **The Holy Spirit plays a major role in setting up encounters— both sending us as witnesses and initiating with seekers.**

from prebelief to belief in Jesus. Acts 8 shows us the wide angle (the whole story) but also zooms in on the interactions Philip had with the Spirit and the unusual encounter he had with the Ethiopian.

Before we dive in to this story, however, I need to state that while Acts 8 is a great description of an evangelistic encounter, it does not prescribe how *every* evangelistic encounter should proceed. My intention is to pull principles from the story that are seen throughout the New Testament. These principles will help us move into awkward encounters more readily and faithfully, allowing us to see God work powerfully in people's lives.

The Spirit Sends

If we were to study Acts 8 with an eye on each character's role in the Ethiopian's conversion, we would find some interesting observations. Every conversion has three players: the Holy Spirit, the witness and the seeker. First, we are going to look at the role of the Spirit in bringing people to faith.

Let's start with what the Spirit does in an observable way in the story.

> Now an angel of the Lord said to Philip, "Go south to the road—the desert road—that goes down from Jerusalem to Gaza." So he started out, and on his way he met an Ethiopian eunuch, an important official in charge of all the treasury of the Kandake (which means "queen of the Ethiopians"). This man had gone to Jerusalem to worship, and on his way home was sitting in his chariot reading the Book of Isaiah the prophet. The Spirit told Philip, "Go to that chariot and stay near it." (Acts 8:26-29)

Acts 8 shows that the Spirit is a sending God. He knew the Ethiopian was on a spiritual journey, was a seeker and needed help interpreting his experience. So the Spirit sent Philip into the mix. Interestingly, Philip had a two-part sending. First, the angel sent Philip in a general direction: "Go south to the road." It wasn't until Philip was on his way down the road that the Spirit sent him in a more specific direction—"Go to that chariot and stay near it."

There is a moment in chess when your opponent makes a great move and you realize he put a particular piece in a particular place earlier in the match as a setup for this move. Likewise, early on God moved Philip in a head-scratching, vague way, only to move him later directly to the target.

Philip was probably confused as to why the Spirit sent him to the desert road going south. He must have had a million questions:

"Why this way?"

"What is down that road?"

"What is God up to?"

"Huh? This makes no sense!"

The Spirit asks us to do these types of things as well. If we don't follow the general directions, we won't see what God specifically had in mind for us next. *Often God sends us in general ways and then reveals the clear reason later.*

One year during our campus ministry, two women in our Inter-Varsity chapter, Alyssa and Aubrey, sensed God ask them to go on the schoolwide leadership retreat. It was for the leaders of campus organizations in general, not a Christian retreat.

Alyssa and Aubrey were not flaming evangelists but more pastoral and shepherding in their gifting. They didn't wake up every day longing for a daring encounter with a stranger. In fact, I don't think either had personally influenced anyone to come to faith.

They obeyed God's nudging to go on the retreat and connect with other leaders at their school, and it didn't take long for God to show them why. On the bus leaving campus, they met Jake. When he asked them what InterVarsity was about, the conversation quickly turned to the chapter's upcoming trip to Catalina Island for spring break.

"This sounds really interesting," Jake said. "Can I come?"

Overjoyed, Alyssa and Aubrey said yes and spent the rest of the retreat building relationship with Jake.

He did go with us to Catalina, where he met God in amazing ways. First, as usual, this week was dedicated to an inductive study of the Gospel of Mark. Jake was able to see Jesus in action, ask questions and wrestle with the text. Second, during a powerful prayer time, he said he could feel the love among people in the room. He wanted to commit his life to Christ, and even asked God how he could be an influence in his fraternity.

I love Jake's story because it shows how God sends people into mission to meet people he is already working with. Furthermore, Alyssa and Aubrey were not gifted in evangelism, but they committed to God's mission. They were so excited that they said yes when God sent them on the retreat because they got to see God work in Jake's life.

It also shows how the witnessing community as a whole is in play. We are not called to witness alone. Aubrey and Alyssa were sent from a community and felt empowered to share their faith and look for opportunities, knowing that when they came back a whole community would be there to help them. And it did. Jake was able to come to faith in Christ not just because of their influence but also the group's pursuit of him for months. If our communities embraced witness more fully, many more people who don't feel gifted in this area would be empowered to step up and out for Jesus.

God Will Show

Some people are not going to show up where you are. The way you will find them is through God's leading you to them. This is the single biggest reason most people do not see others come to faith. They wait for God to make everything clear before they act. However, most of the people I have seen come to faith have done so because I obeyed God to go to a certain place before the person I was to encounter appeared.

When Alyssa and Aubrey got on the bus, it was as if they were in the perfect place at the perfect time. Jake showed up on the bus and was curious about God. But if those two women hadn't first obeyed God to go on the retreat, they might never have met Jake. Jake needed them to meet him in his context, at a leadership retreat. He was not going to wander into a Christian meeting on his own. God's plan that day was to awaken his curiosity on the bus.

You would have agreed to go on the retreat too if you knew Jake would be there and eager to talk. But that's the problem: *God often asks us to go somewhere before we know why.*

Unfortunately, many Christians believe God always gives specific answers and specific directions, so they miss out on much of what he may be saying in general. If something is fuzzy at the start, then we tend to write it off as not of God and move on.

Going back to the previous chapters on spiritual warfare, we tend to be very rational and logical. If something doesn't make sense, we write it off. Many of us tend to be linear thinkers. Following a God who sends us down a desert road with no direction does not make a lot of sense to the Western mindset. We have been trained since birth to ask why, and when the answer isn't clear we tend to rebel. How many times have you said to someone (maybe a parent), "I am not doing that! It makes no sense."

Well, God sends his people to do things that sometimes don't make sense at first. We need to follow his leading like Philip, even if it means going down a dusty road for no apparent reason.

The more I coach others in witness, the more I am concerned for our lack of ability to hear God send us in general ways. If we expect God to make the end clear from the start, we will miss him and truncate the plan he has for us and those we could encounter.

Sending Throughout the Bible

The sending nature of God runs from cover to cover in Scripture. From beginning to end, God sent his people on mission, both in general directions and then in very specific ways. In Genesis 12, Abram was sent to an unknown land (general), and then in Exodus God sent Moses back to his people (specific). In Acts 1 the disciples were sent into the world to be witnesses (general), but then in Acts 10 Peter was sent for a specific encounter with Cornelius (among many other specific encounters God set up).

But in the pinnacle act of God's mission, Jesus was sent to earth to rescue all of humanity. God locates his sending nature in his Son, who not only came to earth to be with sinners but also was sent to the cross to bear the sins of the world. With the resurrection we are sent by the Holy Spirit, and one of his primary jobs is to send us into the world as witnesses.

> When he, the Spirit of truth, comes, he will guide you into all the truth. He will not speak on his own; he will speak only what he hears, and he will tell you what is yet to come. (John 16:13)

> Jesus said, "Peace be with you! As the Father has sent me, I am sending you." And with that he breathed on them and said, "Receive the Holy Spirit." (John 20:21-22)

You will receive power when the Holy Spirit comes on you; and you will be my witnesses in Jerusalem, and in all Judea and Samaria, and to the ends of the earth. (Acts 1:8)

The Spirit is now in your midst and eager to "speak *to you* what he hears" and send you into God's mission. If you are not hearing from the Spirit and allowing him to send you into the Father's plans, then you can neither be an effective witness for Christ nor fulfill your purpose on earth.

Craig Keener in his commentary on the Gospel of John says this,

Whereas the sending of the Son is the heart of the Fourth Gospel's plot, its conclusion is open-ended, spilling into the story of the disciples. Thus the church's mission is, for John's theology, to carry on Jesus' mission (14:12; 17:18). Because Jesus was sending "just as" (*kathos*) the Father sent him (20:21), the disciples would carry on Jesus' mission, including not only signs pointing to Jesus (14:12) but also witness (15:27) through which the Spirit would continue Jesus' presence and work (16:7-11).[1]

Fig. 8.1. Philip deciding whether to obey or to stay in Samaria. Art by Juliano Yi.

God loves humankind and will do anything he can to get us into relationship with him, including sending you and me into mission. We can't make mission a program; it's a way of life. If we are going to make mission a way of life, we have to embrace the reality that sometimes God sends us into things that don't yet make sense. But knowing God is a sending God who has a purpose behind what he does gives us confidence to step out even when we don't know the end of the story. We need to be more like Philip, who actively followed the Spirit even though the purpose was unclear.

The Spirit Initiates

It is clear in Acts 8 that the Spirit had already initiated relationship with the Ethiopian—he was clearly seeking God. The man was curious, was reading Scripture and was waiting for an interpretation. God was working in this man. The Ethiopian had gone to Jerusalem to worship, and on his way home he sat in his chariot reading the book of Isaiah. The Spirit told Philip, "Go to that chariot and stay near it" (v. 29). *It is not the job of a witness to force things in order to make someone believe.* This is one of the greatest lessons I have learned as an evangelist: God is the initiator, and he will make evangelistic encounters happen. In prayer we must wait on God to open people up to himself.

Overeager Christians often try to stir things up on their own and push others into conversations. This is a mistake. On the flip side, less eager Christians worry that unless they are able to conjure up opportunities to witness, they are not meant for evangelism.

When my sister Gina started college the year after I did, we didn't exactly get along well. I had become a Christian the year before, and all I wanted to do was convert her to Christ. She came to the University of San Diego so we could develop our relationship. But I had one thing on my mind, and it quickly annoyed her.

Now that she was away from her high school friends, I saw it as the perfect time to introduce her to Jesus. I constantly talked about Jesus, invited her to InterVarsity events and church, and gave her advice about parties, guys and being in a sorority. It got so bad that Gina asked my campus minister to tell me to stop talking to her about God and to leave her alone. As you can imagine, she did not enjoy being with me.

I had great intentions, but no idea what it meant to let God set up the opportunity to draw her to him. I didn't know, or at least I didn't believe, that God initiates conversion. I thought it was up to me to convert Gina and do all I could to hold the truth in front of her.

"Beau," my campus minister said, "why don't you take your sister out for ice cream and talk to her about something other than God?" He went on to explain that God initiates and draws people to himself. He shared John 6:44, which talks about no one coming to Jesus unless the Father draws them. I realized I needed to back off and let God do his thing. For the rest of the year I gave Gina space. I didn't talk about God unless she brought it up, and I tried to do other fun things with her.

God initiates and draws people to himself.

The next summer I went to Egypt on a missions trip. When I returned, Gina and I decided to play a game of tennis. "I am starting to get more curious about God," Gina said, right in the middle of one of our points, "and I want to talk to you about it."

My jaw dropped. So did my racket. I came up to the net to find out more.

Gina had been talking to a friend from high school while they both were home for the summer. Her friend had made some good points about God. Gina was open now, but still had some qualms. She told me her biggest obstacle to being a Christian was that most Christians her age were boring, and her friends who were fun were neither Christian nor moral.

"If I can find some people who are both fun and Christian," she said, "I would give this a shot."

I looked her in the eye and said, "God will give you those friends. Let me pray now that you would meet them this fall at school."

When we got back to school that fall, two of Gina's sorority sisters asked her to meet weekly to go through a Christian book together. Gina already liked these women, but didn't know they were so serious about their faith. She joined them. Later that year Gina became a Christian, went on a missions trip to India the following summer and ended up being discipled by an older sorority sister for the next two years. (By the way, that sorority sister is now my wife, something else I had no clue God was setting up!)

Gina's story is a fitting example of how we have to wait for God to initiate with people and set up encounters. I am not saying that you should never talk to people first or break the ice in conversations, but you should wait for God's timing when someone doesn't respond well. Unlike the Ethiopian, who was open to conversation and seeking God in Scripture, initially my sister was not prepared. I needed to chill out and wait. I learned an incredible lesson about waiting, watching and praying for God to first move in someone's heart.

Again, this is a great example of how a witnessing community works. It's important that a church or fellowship is on mission together. I played a key part, but not the only part, in Gina coming to faith. It took a group of people to move her along. Sometimes God sends us into someone's life to spark their curiosity; other times it will be to take them all the way to Christ. We just don't know, and that is why we continually need to lean into witness.

Key Step: Take Stock

Write down all the different networks you are in. Spend some time thinking and praying about why God has placed you where you are, and ask him to make you more aware of why he has sent you there. Also ask God if there is anywhere else he may want you to go. Pay attention to individuals that come to mind as you think about where God has sent or is sending you. My prayer is that you get to see people come to faith like

Yoshiko and Gina did. That will require you to step out, follow the Spirit and allow him to set up your encounters.

Reflection Questions

1. Imagine God sending you to someone. How would you feel if God changed someone for eternity through you?

2. What do you like about the Holy Spirit in Acts 8? What did you learn about the Spirit?

3. Do you tend to be too pushy or too timid? Why do you think you're that way?

4. What do you like about being told to relax and wait on God?

5. How does the fear of coming across as pushy stop you from stepping out into the Spirit's leading?

9

Your Role

Follow Even If Fuzzy

I HAD BEEN BUILDING TRUST with some San Diego State students for a while and wanted to spend more time with them. While we were bowling on campus one night, one of them said he was going to a fraternity party later, and I sensed God urging me to go with them. So I spoke up, "Let me roll with you guys." I wanted to model for them being in the world but not of it and show them a different picture of God and of a minister. I thought they would think it was inspiring that a minister would go to a party on campus.

As soon as we got to the party, a guy rushed up to me and said, "Beau, do you remember me? We need to talk now!"

I had met Robert outside the dorms months earlier, but hadn't seen him since. When we first met, I had taken the opportunity to witness to him, but he wasn't open then. The night of the party, however, he was very open. He had recently been in a near-fatal car accident and survived. For two hours he urgently asked questions about God in a corner of the frat house backyard. If I hadn't obeyed God's general direction to go to the party, this specific conversation would not have happened that night.

Follow the General, Anticipate the Specific

Sometimes God asks us to move to a new city or quit our current job, though we don't know why at the time. Other times he may ask us to take a walk in a different direction or hang out a little longer in a certain place. These are general things we sense from God, but the specific reason is not yet clear.

I talk to many people who say they are not evangelists or not gifted in leading people to the Lord. But when I go deeper with them, it's not that they lack special gifting but they won't let God put them into different situations in a general sense. Being an effective evangelist means obeying the Spirit as he tells us to do something in a general sense so we can see why he was sending us specifically. When we allow God to speak to us generally and with anticipation of specific direction, we will soon see why we were sent somewhere or to someone.

Philip: The Role of the Witness

So far, we've looked at the Spirit's role pertaining to the conversion process. Now, we turn our attention to the witness's role. In Acts 8 the Spirit sent Philip and initiated the Ethiopian's conversion process, but Philip had a crucial role to play as well.

To feel the magnitude of Philip's responsibility in response to the Spirit sending him, look at table 9.1, which lists the things the Spirit and Philip did.

Table 9.1

The Spirit (Sender)	Philip (Witness)
Said to go south	Obeyed general direction to go south
Said to go to the chariot	Ran up to the chariot
Stayed silent	Heard the Ethiopian reading Asked the Ethiopian a question Went into the chariot when invited Explained the good news Baptized the Ethiopian
Took Philip away	Kept preaching in new location

Notice that Philip's list is longer than the Spirit's. (We will soon discuss why the Spirit initiates the process but seems to go silent once the seeking Ethiopian shows up!) As a modern-day witness, you may feel that Philip's list is overwhelming. When I teach this material in my seminar, I often feel the tension rise in the room as people realize the witness's list is large. I imagine inner voices of inadequacy and fear whispering, *Don't mess this up. This is too big for you. Can you really do this? You'll have to talk to people, and ask good questions, and share the gospel in a relevant way, and lead them to faith in Jesus, and baptize them.*

True, it is a lot to handle. Responding to the Spirit's direction has significant responsibilities. But let's suspend these feelings for a moment and instead say, *I know this is a lot, but I am up for the challenge.* Then most people jump right to, *Okay, train me in what to say and how to do this!* And though that is probably why you are reading this book, you may not be able to go there immediately. You have to address your level of obedience before you work toward a new level of practical training.

> **You have to address your level of obedience before you work toward a new level of practical training.**

Six Important Steps

Philip is a great example of someone who obeys the Spirit's prompting to move before understanding why. His ongoing relationship and conversation with God shows how important it is to be in tune with the Spirit in our everyday life so we won't miss directions from God, especially directions that make no sense at first.

Here's a chronological outline of the interactions between the Spirit, Philip and the Ethiopian:

1. An angel tells Philip to go south down the desert road.

2. Philip heads down the desert road without any idea why.

3. The Spirit directs Philip to stand near the chariot.

4. Philip runs to the chariot.

5. Philip listens and overhears the Ethiopian reading Scripture.

6. Philip uses his own discernment, and asks the Ethiopian a question.

7. The Ethiopian responds and invites Philip into the chariot.

8. The Ethiopian asks a question.

9. Philip explains the good news.

10. The Ethiopian believes and is baptized.

11. Philip is taken away by the Spirit.

Fig. 9.1. Philip encountering the Ethiopian. Art by Juliano Yi.

There are six steps that happen between Philip and the Spirit before the Ethiopian responds, and four steps before the Ethiopian shows up on the scene. The point here is that many of our witnessing opportunities are being set up by the Spirit. How we interact with the Spirit and obey his directions will determine whether we encounter the person. It is amazing how God used Philip to lead the Ethiopian to faith, but it is also quite sobering to realize that the Ethiopian didn't show up in Philip's world. Philip had to be moved by the Spirit to the Ethiopian. Philip's obedience to a seemingly illogical direction was crucial.

You may not be seeing breakthroughs in the places you live and work. One reason may be that you aren't as in tune with the Spirit as you are called to be. For instance, when was the last time you stopped to ask the Spirit where you should go or with whom you should start a conversation? When was the last time the Spirit prompted you to talk with someone, but you ignored it because it felt uncomfortable? Those are not training problems. Those are obedience problems. Similarly, many Christians are waiting for a person to show up on their turf, when God is trying to send them to the person.

For now, try to suspend any nervousness about how to have a spiritual conversation, and acknowledge that obedience to God's directions is foremost. If

Many Christians are waiting for a person to show up on their turf, when God is trying to send them to the person.

you are thinking to yourself, *It's not that easy!* then you probably feel the same way Philip felt. Put yourself in his shoes and see how staggering this encounter would have been to Philip's faith. In the beginning of Acts 8, Philip was busy in Samaria, casting out demons, preaching and leading people to Jesus. The town was essentially experiencing a revival. Philip was right in the middle of the action, and his ministry dreams were coming alive. But then the Spirit called him to leave all that and head down a rarely traveled desert road. It may have been confusing and frustrating to receive that word. Furthermore, it would have been understandable to think, *This can't be God. God is moving powerfully where I am right now.* It would have been easy for Philip to disregard this word as a weird thought that accidentally popped into his head.

But Philip knew the voice of God and that God's mission is bigger than any one city. Philip must have also seen himself as a free agent for God to use wherever he pleased. It is almost as if Philip just wanted to be part of God's plan to save the world and would go and do whatever was asked of him. He knew it was God talking. And when God said it was time to move, Philip knew it was time to move.

When I think about this context and how strange this must have felt to Philip, it makes me ask some *how* questions. How was Philip able to leave a thriving ministry for a desert road? How was Philip able to hear the Lord call him to such a thing? I feel as if on many days I wouldn't be able to entertain such a thought because it makes no sense.

The following are a few reasons why Philip was able to follow in obedience.

Philip lived by faith. Some theologians comment that God was testing Philip's faith here. God was testing Philip's obedience to move even when it seemed that, unlike his current spot in Samaria, there wouldn't be anyone to preach to in the barren desert. Just as God called Abram to an unknown land, he was testing Philip to see if he would follow.

Hebrews 11:1 says, "Now faith is confidence in what we hope for and assurance about what we do not see." God's call to Philip didn't make sense in light of his active ministry in Samaria, but Philip left because he knew God. His faith was rooted in God's character. He was certain that God sends his people.

Philip didn't hope that; he had hope in. Philip doesn't move an inch without great hope in Christ and the certainty that Jesus was alive and was working in this new place. Philip was able to move from a thriving ministry in Samaria to a barren desert road because the Spirit was in both places. Even though Philip couldn't see anything happening down that desert road, he didn't assume God wasn't up to something. Philip didn't follow Jesus because of results; he followed Jesus because he wanted to be where Jesus was. He knew that because Jesus was calling him, things would happen—even in a barren place—because Jesus was there.

I'm not encouraging you to a life which hopes *that* God will show up in the next place, but that hopes *in* the God who shows up. Your hope is in a sending God who creates encounters with other people. Your hope is in the resurrected Christ creating kingdom moments out of nothing. Even if Jesus calls you to seemingly barren places, I pray you will go with hope in Christ. I want you to be the kind of person that says, "I want to go wherever God calls me, even if it looks bleak, because I want to be where he is moving."

Philip didn't follow Jesus because of results; he followed Jesus because he wanted to be where Jesus was.

Philip knew who owned the ministry. The other reason Philip was able to leave quickly when the Spirit called is that he knew who owned his ministry: not him but God alone. Philip was experiencing breakthrough in Samaria and likely felt highly validated in his call to ministry. Things were bursting at the seams, and probably the last thought on Philip's mind was, *This would be a great time to leave.*

But Philip was God's man in God's game. He must have had a healthy perspective: a huge view of God and a small view of himself. Not a small view of himself in a limiting way but one in which he was a player on a team with God as the coach and the owner. Philip knew he was an important part of the team, but when the coach said it was time to switch positions, who was Philip to argue? If the owner wanted to trade him to another part of the country, who was Philip to object?

Are you like Philip in this way? Are you able to see God as the owner of your ministry and yourself as a player? If God wanted to move you out of your city, your church, your work, your campus or your current job, would you be able to hear his call?

I contend that one of the primary reasons some Christians can't hear God's call is because they feel they own the ministry: *It would fall apart without us.* (Or maybe we would fall apart.) We become the center. We become the god.

It was only a few years ago I had to face this reality. I was leading the ministry at San Diego State when God unexpectedly made it clear it was time to leave. Our ministry was doing well, and I didn't want to go. I didn't have to leave either. But after several conversations with my mentors about the sense I was getting from God, it was clear that my wife and I were supposed to leave San Diego to pursue a different opportunity with God.

I had been in San Diego for eleven years, and my wife for fourteen. It was sad for us to think about moving. Adding to the craziness, we had bought a house a few years before and were expecting our second child in a month. We didn't think we could sell our house for what we bought it for, and moving shortly after having a baby seemed ridiculous.

One afternoon in our living room, we were praying and talking with a few of our mentors, and God made it clear it was time to go. These particular mentors were in their fifties and had better perspective than we did, being in our thirties. They were also, in our minds, our most conservative mentors. We were wholeheartedly expecting them to encourage us to stay in San Diego. But of all the people praying for us about the move, in prayer they heard the word of Abram being called to an unfamiliar land. After prayer, one of them looked at me and said as directly as he could, "You can't stay here. God is calling you onward."

The next day we called the leader of our ministry and told him we were leaving San Diego at the end of the year. The only problem was that we had no idea where we were going. We just knew we were going.

This was the craziest time of living by faith in my life. We had our baby, sold our house (for what we bought it for and in only two weeks!), found the right rental and moved to Los Angeles. This all happened—from sensing God's call to moving—in three months. We were heading to a city my wife dreaded going to and I wasn't crazy about either.

It was a wild ride with a lot of bumps along the way. But both of us can say today that it was a great move. We said the other day that we can't imagine still being in San Diego. God has shown us why we are here: to start new things with him on college campuses all over LA. And, wouldn't you know, San Diego State is doing just fine without us too!

You Want Me to Say What?

During my junior year of college, I was following the Spirit down the general path of "What will I do when I graduate?" I regularly asked God to make things specific, and here I was asking him to show me whether I should go into business or campus ministry.

I loved business. I grew up in a very entrepreneurial family. I had worked in international trade in China for a summer during college, was nearly fluent in Chinese and potentially could land a job in China.

My oldest brother, Fred, was part of an organization called Young Presidents Organization. To be in YPO, you had to be less than fifty and be the president of a company that did at least $10 million in sales per year. To introduce me to the presidents of companies ranging in sales from $10 million to $500 million, Fred took me to one of their networking dinners during my junior year. It was a fantastic opportunity, to say the least. We spent about an hour schmoozing and socializing. Fred introduced me to people and talked me up. It was great, but then it got uncomfortable.

Everyone I met asked what I wanted to do after graduation, so I told them my dreams for business. But at one point I heard the Holy Spirit whisper to me, clear as day, "Tell the next person that you are a Christian and considering ministry."

You want me to say what? I thought. *No, God! This is weird.*

My brother is not a Christian, and the networking event was not religious at all. God had to be kidding me. I felt so nervous, but I was also ready to be obedient to Jesus. And the next thing that crossed my mind was that maybe the next person was ready to accept Jesus. Perhaps God was setting me up to lead that person to faith.

Obediently and nervously, when the man I met next said, "So, Beau, what is it that you want to do when you graduate?" I told him, "Well, I know this is kind of strange to say at an event like this, but I am considering Christian ministry." Gulp.

To my surprise, the multimillionaire businessman punched me in the shoulder and said, "No way! That is awesome. I am a believer too!"

I was shocked and elated. This man was genuinely excited that I was a believer, and he even invited me to sit at his table for dinner!

The table was loaded with five Christian friends. I couldn't believe how the trajectory of my night had changed: I was sitting with six very successful Christian businessmen, and they were asking me about my passions and dreams. As I told them about my passion to minister to people and share the gospel, they were convinced that I should say yes to ministering to college students. One man in particular said, "You will always have business to come back to when you are older, but it is clear you are passionate about the campus, and it seems God is calling you there. You should do that, and we will support you."

But what sealed the deal for me was the question, "What would you rather have: one thousand employees or one thousand disciples?" The man who asked this told me that he loved business and sees it as his calling, but he works hard at it every day and it takes all his time. While he gets opportunities to minister to people here and there, being a successful businessman means working hard at business. My heart jumped—I immediately knew I wanted disciples. I told him so, and the whole table resounded, "Go into ministry, kid."

Being on InterVarsity staff requires that I raise support for the ministry, and all six men invested in me financially as I got started. Not only did God use that networking event to speak to me about ministry in an unlikely place, he gave me a support team as well.

I love this story because through all my praying about what I should do after college, God made it clear. But the direct step God asked me to take to find that clarity was very uncomfortable and strange. I wanted him to make it clear what I should do, but I wasn't expecting him to make it clear that I needed to bring up ministry at a high-powered networking event. That prompt was shocking. But, of course, the man on the receiving end was open and the perfect person to help me get to the next step in the Lord's plan.

As I look back on experiences when God led me down a certain path of faith, the point where things became clear often seemed counter-intuitive and filled with tension. If we expect the moment of clarity to make things easier, we are setting up ourselves for disappointment and the potential to miss God. Instead, clarity often produces more awkward times, but we need to move through the moment with obedience so we can see God break through.

> **If we expect the moment of clarity to make things easier, we are setting up ourselves for disappointment and the potential to miss God.**

Three Common Barriers

As you become a person who walks by faith into both the general and specific directions the Spirit gives you, a few fears or barriers may come up even if you recognize that God has spoken to you.

1. I'm worried God won't show up. Many times when I debrief people about why they didn't act on what they sensed God saying to them, they say they were scared that God wouldn't show up.

Yes, it would be embarrassing to step out for God and he didn't show up. While I can't promise you that you won't hear that from others from time to time, I *can* promise you that when God asks his people to step out, he will back them up.

My friend John Teter, talking about the Gospel of John, said this in his book *Get the Word Out*:

Whenever a witness would go before Jesus, preparing the way by declaring the words of life to a group of people, Jesus would then physically follow that witness to personally visit the people. Seven times he spent time with the people personally, and the spiritual impact was invariably the same: the result of Jesus' follow-up was genuine faith and the conversion of the hearers, and deepening of the witnesses' faith.[1]

Jesus doesn't leave his witnesses abandoned. He will follow you up. And if he is calling you to a new place, albeit unclear or confusing, he will back you up the same way he did Philip.

2. *I have a lot going on here!* Most of us aren't sitting around looking for more things to do. We have friends, families and full schedules. And if we are part of a ministry, we already have people we are caring for or trying to reach, so what could God possibly want with us somewhere else?

However, we see in Acts 8 and many other places in Scripture that God does call people to drop what they are doing and go elsewhere, start something new or encounter someone looking for God. We must be careful to not assume that God wouldn't call us because we are busy or otherwise productive. He may call us to change jobs or leave a city right when things are at their peak. He may ask us to cancel an appointment to pursue another opportunity that is unclear. It is not against his nature to send busy people to less busy places, and it wouldn't be smart to say, "Sorry, God, I can't. I have a lot going on here!"

3. *I don't know enough to share.* People often tell me, "I don't know how to share my faith" or "I don't have all the tools to do it well. I need to learn more." But this can be a paralyzing lie that keeps us from moving with God.

When we listen to God and obey his directions, the tools will kick in. God often calls witnesses somewhere before they know what to say or how to say it. God regularly calls people who don't have all the right tools.[2]

If you sense God is calling you somewhere, but you keep telling yourself, *I don't know enough yet, so that must not be God,* then you are limiting what God may be doing. God will equip you for the task once you're there. He will help you understand what to say or how to act once he shows you exactly why you are there. So, when you sense God's prompting to take a risk and follow him, move whether you are well trained or not.

In fact, it is Jesus' character to send people who are not prepared and then give them exactly what they need when they're on the hot seat. For example, in Matthew 10:18-20, Jesus says, "On my account you will be brought before governors and kings as witnesses to them and to the Gentiles. But when they arrest you, do not worry about what to say or how to say it. At that time you will be given what to say, for it will not be you speaking, but the Spirit of your Father speaking through you."

Philip wasn't successful because he led the Ethiopian to the Lord. He was successful because he followed the Spirit down a desert road, which made no sense. God called, and Philip followed. That's faith. That's pleasing to God.

My prayer is that we will follow God and be obedient to his call no matter how crazy or confusing the call may be, no matter if the time is right or not. God has people waiting for us, and we need to move in step with him in order for God to reach them.

Key Step: Pay Attention to God's Leading

Pay attention to a general leading from God this week. Is he asking you to call someone whom you hadn't even had on your mind? Is he asking you to strike up a conversation with someone at work you don't usually talk with? Take a moment this week and ask God if there is somewhere he wants you to go or someone he wants you to talk to who was not originally in your plan.

Reflection Questions

1. What do you admire about Philip?

2. How can you begin to regularly (daily or weekly) ask the Holy Spirit to make you more sensitive to him?

3. Describe a time when you had to do something that didn't make sense in your ordinary routine.

4. How do you feel about God interrupting your routine? Why?

10

Don't Miss the Moment

I WAS DEBRIEFING WITH two small group leaders when a very interesting thing happened. Like I always do, I asked them how the Bible study went and if anything in particular stood out to them. As the two leaders were explaining their interactions, it became increasingly clear to me that Jenny, a woman in their group, was ready to start following Jesus. I could tell by the way they were describing Jenny's questions and how she had interacted with the group.

"So you asked Jenny if she was ready to start following Jesus, right?" I asked.

"No," they said, and nervously laughed as though I was suggesting they take a round trip to Mars. They said they thought that it would be weird to bring that up in the group, and they didn't think Jenny was ready to follow Jesus.

I always give my leaders the benefit of the doubt, and I trusted their judgment in particular. But I could sense their fear, so I asked one more question: "Are you scared to ask Jenny if she is ready to follow Jesus, or do you *really* think she is not ready? Be honest."

Full of nerves, they chuckled again and one said, "Well, I think we are just scared. But we don't really think she is ready anyways. I mean, don't you think she would have told us if she was ready?"

We will pick up this story later, but this is a great place to acknowledge these tensions. Two major things were happening as these women were discerning whether Jenny was ready to start following Jesus.

   1. *Assuming the seeker will bring up the time to make a decision.* These leaders were assuming that Jenny would tell them when she was ready to follow Jesus. But most seekers are not going to simply say, "I am ready to follow Jesus." They don't know how to do this; it's foreign to them. They don't know to ask, "Can I enter into the kingdom of God? Can I repent of my sins now?" They don't have the language to ask these things. Seekers may have strong stirrings in their heart and soul, and they may be able to sense that God is close, but they don't know how to articulate starting a relationship with Jesus. If we wait for a seeker to bring it up, we will wait for a long time. Instead, we have to ask seekers the right questions and give them a chance to respond.

   I don't know anything about cars, but I can always tell when my car is acting strange. Last year I was driving down the freeway when my car started to shake and make funny noises. I was able to drive it for a while, but it soon became too difficult. If you had asked me about it at that time, I would not have said, "Dang, I need a new catalytic converter. I better get to a mechanic." I had no idea. I just knew something was up. As soon as a trusted mechanic told me what I needed, I accepted the news and moved forward.

   Many of our friends are like this. They know something isn't working, but they aren't spiritual experts. They don't know how to diagnose their spiritual life, and they don't know what they need to do to make it happen. That they will inform you they need Christ or want to start a relationship with him is as likely as my ability to diagnose my car's mechanical problem. I had to explain to these two leaders that they are like spiritual mechanics, and that they could always ask at the end of small group, "Does anyone here want to start a relationship with Jesus tonight?"

   Be a bold but gentle spiritual mechanic with the people in your life. Tell them what they need to hear. Tell them what is wrong and how to fix it. They may never figure it out without your help.

2. *Living in fear.* It is important to be aware of our fear and how it is working in us. This is a major struggle in sharing the faith.

These group leaders didn't ask Jenny to start following Jesus because *they* were scared. Jenny never said *she* was scared. In this case the leaders let their fear control them, and they ended up saying no on Jenny's behalf.

How many times has God given you a witnessing moment to step into, but because of fear you said no for the person God led you to?

I was surprised to run into an old friend at my church a few years ago. When I went to talk with him, I could see he was on fire in his faith. I asked him how he became a Christian, and he said he had recently started following Jesus thanks to a friend at work. I will never forget what he said next. He told me he had been curious throughout college, but no one helped him find his way. He wasn't saying this to me in a complaining or victimized way, but more like, "Hey, I was open, more open than I realized. But I think everyone wrote me off as too far away or closed. People said no for me instead of letting me say no myself." I left that time with him and vowed never to assume someone wasn't ready. I need to explore people's curiosity no matter how far from God they appear to be.

Go Back

As the two nervous leaders told me they were scared, I had a moment of compassion for them. I looked them in the eyes and told them I understood their fear and that it was normal. I told them I saw where they were coming from, but that none of us can let fear lead us and determine our course of action.

I told them that I thought Jenny was open to following Jesus and needed an invitation since she didn't know how to invite herself into the kingdom of God. Then, I told them they needed to go to where Jenny lives and explain to her that they thought they made a mistake, and that there was a step to take that couldn't wait until next week. "We can't miss this moment!" I told them. Jenny was open, and God was giving them a moment to step into right then.

The leaders looked at me awkwardly, laughed again and asked, "Are you sure?"

At this point, you may think, "Beau, that's a bit extreme. There's no way I would go back to Jenny right away." I can understand why you would feel that way.

All I can say is that I was sure Jenny was ready to follow Jesus and I didn't want these leaders to miss the moment.

When you know someone is ready and you discern the time is right, you have to step in as a witness, no matter how weird it is. Philip was standing next to a stranger's chariot, for crying out loud! The least we can do is go back and visit a person from our small group with whom we have already built trust. Furthermore, the best gift we can ever receive as a witness is seeing someone say yes to following Jesus. I wanted these leaders to share in the incredible joy of seeing someone come to faith, so I encouraged them to go back.[1]

> When you know someone is ready and you discern the time is right, you have to step in as a witness, no matter how weird it is.

I told the leaders that we would meet in thirty minutes, but that I wanted them to find Jenny and say the following to her: "Jenny, you seemed really curious about Jesus tonight, even more so than other weeks. As we were thinking about it, we thought you might be ready to start a relationship with him. We thought you might not really know how to do that or even ask for that if you did want that. Is that true?"

They went on their way to deliver the message. Full of fear, worry and anticipation, the women surprisingly found Jenny very open. They said what I told them to say, and Jenny lit up. "Yes," she said, "it is true." Jenny told them that she really did want to follow Jesus, she just didn't know how. She was so thankful that the leaders had come back.

Meanwhile, I was waiting for the leaders to return. They soon came storming back in the door and screamed with joy that Jenny had decided to follow Jesus. The leaders, laughing again, were full of joy and wonder this time. They couldn't believe it. We had another excellent time debriefing as we talked about discerning moments and not missing these moments when God is setting them up. For the next hour we discussed how to gauge curiosity and ask the question, and that we have to be led by faith rather than fear. It was such a great night!

This too reveals that witnessing communities are the best. These women were partners in leading an evangelistic Bible study, and I was their coach. My role was to coach, encourage and infuse faith and boldness into them. But as followers of Jesus, they were called to witness and lead others to faith.

God Creates, We Respond

The reality of being a witness is that God sets up moments between his witnesses and seekers. It is our job to step into these moments and share the gospel. We don't have to create the moments; we only need to respond to them.

When I train others on sharing Jesus and turning awkward moments into breakthroughs, I am often asked, "Won't God tell me when it is time to speak? I mean, if he is leading me into these moments, won't he make it clear when to open my mouth?"

Not necessarily.

Philip was led down the desert road and to the chariot by the Spirit. But once he was there and overheard the Ethiopian reading, his discernment kicked in and he realized he needed to interject. Philip seized the moment, but the text does not say that the Spirit told him to speak.

Recently, as we were driving home from a party, my neighbor confessed to me that he was addicted to alcohol. He had been trying to quit drinking for the last month, and then at the party he pounded three beers. On the way home he felt bad about it, so he opened up.

Of course I listened first, and we had a great talk about addiction and the need for AA. I also was able to share with him some of my background with addiction in my family.

It would have been very easy to keep it at that. It was an intense conversation, and I was a good friend for him in the moment. But I knew God wanted to do more. I wasn't satisfied leaving the man depressed by his powerlessness, with only the hope of AA. So I took a risk and spoke up: "Have you ever considered where God may be in this? I know you want to change, and you want to be free of these inner demons. The best way I know how that can happen is the power of God. He can change you. Are you open to talking about how he could show up in your life and help you?" He turned to me and said, "I want that. I just need to get over what my wife will think if I turn to religion. But I have been thinking about that lately."

The risk of bringing up Jesus paid off. My neighbor even texted me later that night: "Thanks for the conversation." I offered to go to an AA meeting with him and help him with whatever he needs. We are going to continue our talks about God. I am hopeful going forward with my neighbor.

As a witness, we have to use our faith and discernment to realize why we are where we are, assume God is up to something, and at the first sign of spiritual interest press in and speak.

John 4

A great example of this is in John 4. Jesus "had" to go to Samaria, and when he was there he met the woman at the well, who was far from God. But Jesus knew why he was there and he pressed in. He engaged her in conversation, and a dynamic spiritual interaction occurred.

You likely know the story: Jesus gave the woman a prophetic word and revealed to her that he was the Messiah. The woman believed in him, returned home and testified to her village. A broken, outcast woman became the vehicle of transformation for the whole town. Jesus had one spiritual conversation with the least likely person and flipped a whole village upside down. But where were Jesus' disciples? In verse 8 the text says, "His disciples had gone into the town to buy food." They missed the conversation Jesus had with the woman at the well.

Every time I read this passage, I think about how much they missed and how sad it must have made Jesus. There is no doubt why Jesus says,

> My food . . . is to do the will of him who sent me and to finish his work. Don't you have a saying, "It's still four months until harvest"? I tell you, open your eyes and look at the fields! They are ripe for harvest. Even now the one who reaps draws a wage and harvests the crop for eternal life, so that the sower and the reaper may be glad together. Thus the saying "One sows and another reaps" is true. I sent you to reap what you have not worked for. Others have done the hard work, and you have reaped the benefits of their labor. (vv. 34-38)

The disciples missed the moment, and they didn't understand what happened. They neither understood spiritual food nor that the harvest is now. They had just come back from town, and all they had brought was food; the woman was coming back from the town and bringing with her the townspeople to meet Jesus. Jesus was saying, "Open your eyes! This woman, and this whole town, needed to be harvested, and you didn't see it. You thought harvest time was later. Wrong, it is now." The disciples missed the harvest in Samaria because it didn't make sense. "She's just a woman, a non-Jew, an outcast. Ah, let's go to lunch. There's nothing here for us."

But Jesus saw the opportunity and pressed in. Jesus didn't stop because the disciples went to lunch; he kept talking with the woman. The woman saw the opportunity and was a witness to her whole town. They welcomed Jesus with open arms.

Let's reflect on the genesis of awkwardness, which we talked about in chapter three. When social rules are broken, awkwardness is created. Talking to strangers, doing things that are uncomfortable and pressing people on the truth is not socially acceptable. The more we do this, the more we make things awkward. But we haven't addressed what we do because of this reality.

Undoubtedly we would say we avoid the awkward because we are scared and don't want to put ourselves in that kind of tension. But even more obvious than our fear is our lack of compassion. My friend Ram shared this insight with me and it really struck. *We don't avoid the awkward because of fear but because of lack of compassion for people.*

We miss moments with God and others because we don't have compassion for their souls and well-being with God. The disciples checked out and missed a significant moment not because they were scared but because they lacked compassion for Samaritans. Jesus didn't. He knew what they needed. Therefore he pressed in and broke all three rules: (1) he talked to a stranger, (2) he had to have felt a bit uncomfortable, and (3) he pressed her about what was real and true. The moment with the woman at the well was awkward—especially as the encounter started. But Jesus badly wanted the woman to know he was the Messiah, so it was worth it.

How many encounters are you missing with Jesus? Where is Jesus pressing into your neighborhood, office, campus or team? Where does Jesus "have" to go, but you are out to lunch? Powerful breakthrough moments are waiting to happen, but are you "out to lunch" instead?

Friends, please don't miss any more moments with Jesus.

Carolyn and Lu

When Carolyn moved to Santa Monica after graduating from college, she had every reason to focus on her new job in marketing and on making friends. But when she got word that Lu, a woman in her office, was looking for God, she made time to minister to her.

Lu came from a Buddhist background and was currently visiting psychics. She needed answers, was stressed and felt hopeless. Her psychologist, Buddhism, work, boyfriend and even psychics were of no help. She quickly realized they had nothing to offer. But Carolyn was ready to help Lu, and Lu accepted Christ during their first meeting. She was desperate and hungry for something real, and God showed Carolyn that her role was to interpret what was happening to Lu and fill in the rest of the story with the gospel to reveal what God was doing.

Within the first month of moving to Santa Monica, Carolyn had led a colleague to the Lord and altered this woman's eternal destiny and life on earth. Shortly after, Carolyn joined our church, and then Lu did too. It was so great to hear Lu's testimony and to watch Carolyn baptize her as our church shared in the joyous occasion.

Two months after Lu's conversion, she had to return to China to renew her work visa. Within two weeks, she emailed Carolyn that she had led her cousin to faith. God was on the move.

Carolyn's story is a great example of being ready to take advantage of the moments God sets up. We never know who will come to faith and how they may head back to their village and lead others to Jesus too.

Key Step: Examine

Take some time to reflect and pray. Is God working in any relationships in your life but you are missing the signs?

Reflection Questions

1. How would you feel if you were the small group leaders mentioned in this chapter and Beau told you to go back to Jenny?

2. How comfortable are you starting and carrying on conversations with people?

3. Think about a time when you missed a moment. Why did you miss it? What would you counsel yourself to do if you could go back and talk to yourself at that point?

A WITNESS AT WORK

Down the Young Professional Road

Carolyn Chow, account management, advertising

As a recent graduate in the crazy world of advertising, Carolyn Chow is in a bit of transition. "I'm trying to figure out real life and my first 'big girl' job, but also trying to follow Jesus and bring the kingdom of God into my secular workplace." With the "work hard, play even harder" mentality there, she's got quite a challenge before her. Carolyn and I talk about it all the time. How do you reach people with the gospel as an entry-level, minority, twenty-two-year-old woman? Being evangelistic at work means putting a lot at risk: jeopardizing friendships, the work environment and even her livelihood. So it's understandable why at times she feels awkward, insecure and frightened.

But Carolyn has been able to manage life with her coworkers, being present to their complicated lives to encourage and love them without any agenda. Many opportunities to share the gospel and her faith have come up in her short career. "I feel," she says, "like I'm sitting in the tension of my work community being unreached and my hopes for the kingdom of God to break in, and I know I'm called to be a bridge here."

Carolyn recognizes that bringing up Jesus is natural when a person of love and eternal perspective participates in the grind of her coworkers' lives. "If you are truly doing life with friends," she says, "love will naturally move you to share the love and hope of Jesus."

11

How Do I Avoid Being Pushy?

I DID NOT GROW UP IN A CHRISTIAN FAMILY, so when I became a follower of Jesus I wanted to get my whole family onboard. My dad soon accepted Jesus, and so did my sister, but not my mom.

I remember one conversation at a restaurant where I was giving Mom the whole Jesus shebang. I couldn't stand that she wouldn't accept Jesus into her life, so I was trying every angle I could. In that one meal, I covered heaven and hell, sin and salvation, evidence for the resurrection, and the difference between Buddhism and Christianity. I was totally leaning in, and Mom was totally leaning out. She said to me, "Beau, give it a rest. I don't believe this stuff like you do." I wouldn't take no for an answer, and that prevented me from talking about anything else with her that day.

I also remember having coffee with a seeker friend of mine who complained that Christians turned her off. For example, she had a Christian roommate who constantly preached at her. She confessed that she didn't want to follow Jesus if that was what you had to do. "Why can't Christians be normal?" she wondered.

I highly doubt you want to be like I was with my mom or like my friend's roommate. And if you are being totally honest, you often don't share your faith for fear that you may come across like this. The last thing you want is to be perceived as the "pushy Christian."

Suspend Your Negative View

For the remainder of this book, we'll look at how to turn casual conversations into eternal encounters. But you need to first suspend your negative view of evangelists, and ask God to help you embrace a new one. I am not advocating an aggressive, convert-you-at-all-costs type of evangelism.

I know you have seen many horrible examples of evangelism, and I am sorry for that. My prayer, however, is that you ask God to help you suspend your negative view and to show you a new way as we go forward. I want to present you with a way to be relational, tactful, conversational, bold and inviting all at once. It is possible to be a witness like this and see people come to faith. It is also possible to have people thank you for talking with them even when they do not agree with you.

After leading a training session on this material, a man thanked me: "Beau, you showed me a new attitude I can embrace when sharing my faith. I have such a negative image of the evangelist in my head, and you showed me through your stories and training how I can be friends with people, but also intentional and loving with the gospel. I realize now that I need to repent of my negative view and take up this different demeanor. I can be an effective witness to people in my life, and I have a few guys with whom God is inviting me to be intentional."

My hope is that you can have a similar experience.

Is Philip Pushy or Bold?

Was Philip pushy or bold with the Ethiopian? This is one of my favorite questions to ask in my seminar on turning casual conversations into eternal ones. The room usually has a mixed response. The Ethiopian came to faith and seemed to be happy about the experience, but on the other hand, Philip started the conversation, ran up to the chariot, interrupted the guy's day and ended up in the chariot! That seems pushy! However, the room usually lands on the fact that Philip was bold rather than pushy, but they don't know why.

So, what is the difference between being pushy and being bold? The following steps help us differentiate the two.

Step 1: Break the ice. "Philip ran up to the chariot and heard the man reading Isaiah the prophet. 'Do you understand what you are reading?' Philip asked" (Acts 8:30). It is never pushy to discern the moment or ask great questions. This point is often contested in my seminars, but Philip was not being pushy when he overheard the Ethiopian reading Scripture and asked a question.

When God sends us on our way as a witness and sets up an encounter, we have to size up the moment. We have to check the spiritual temperature and see if the person we are going to engage is curious or not. It may be awkward or uncomfortable to ask someone a question out of the blue, but it is not pushy. It is bold.

Think about it as a continuum (see fig. 11.1). A *bold person* will ask a question to break the ice. A *pushy person* asks a question to start a conversation that he or she intends to dominate. A *timid person* perceives someone's openness but avoids engaging him or her.

Timid |—————————— **Patient/Bold** ——————————| **Pushy**

Fig. 11.1. Boldness continuum

Step 2: Test the curiosity level. "'How can I,' [the Ethiopian] said, 'unless someone explains it to me?' So he invited Philip to come up and sit with him" (Acts 8:31). Both bold people and pushy people break the ice and gauge interest, but pushy people reveal themselves in this next step.

When we ask a question or start a conversation, the important factor is how the seeker responds. The seeker will reveal whether he or she is open and curious or closed and skeptical. This makes all the difference.

Bold people move forward when the door opens, and close the conversation down when the door is closed. They don't force a conversation on someone. Pushy people move forward even when the door seems closed. As one of my mentors says, "Boldness without discernment is just muscle." When we feel like it is now or never or that we don't have the luxury to discern the openness of the person, we are being pushy. Bold people are more than happy to move forward if the door is open, but don't feel the need to push.

Two brothers I work with, Kurt Thiel and Larry Thiel, compare the conversation to a train ride. They assume that the conversation (train) is going all the way to the gospel (destination). Kurt and Larry never stop the conversation (train) unless the person they are talking to wants off. They are bold and go all the way to the gospel as the seeker keeps inviting them deeper. But they are also patient. If the person wants off the train and out of the conversation, they willingly shut down the dialogue. *Patience means waiting on God's timing once we break the ice and the person is not open.*

Obviously, in Acts 8 Philip is being bold when he asks the ice-breaking question and then moves into the chariot when the Ethiopian responds favorably and invites Philip in.

Two Helpful Scenarios

Scenario 1. I was walking my dog when one of my neighbors asked me what I do for a living: "Are you a rocket scientist or something?" I laughed and said, "No, I am a Christian minister." He was surprised and said he had never gone to church before. He told me he was a Buddhist and knew nothing about Christianity.

He kept asking me questions as we walked together, so I took the next *bold* step. I asked him if he would like to come to my place later that night, and I could explain more to him about Christianity. He said yes, and we ended up having a great conversation.

Boldness, in this case, came after discerning my neighbor's openness through the ease of our conversation and then inviting him to my house. I saw the open door and boldly took the next step with confidence.

If I had been timid, however, I would have let the conversation fall flat or even changed the subject. Being pushy was not an option because my neighbor showed that he was open.

Remember, the way I am defining *pushy* is continuing to move forward or muscle someone against his or her will.

Scenario 2. I was invited to play golf with a guy I had never talked at length with and I knew was not a Christian. But I also knew that talking with him for four hours on the golf course would give us ample time to talk about Jesus, if he wanted that. We both love sports and share a passion for the Seattle Seahawks.

Halfway through the round, I asked him about his beliefs. "You know I am a Christian. What do you believe about God and faith?"

He explained some things about his views, telling me his wife was Buddhist and he is agnostic. I then said, "Hey, man, if you ever want to talk more about faith and what it means to follow Jesus, I would love to do that with you. What do you think?" He immediately responded, "I am not into that, but thanks." So I turned the conversation back to the Seahawks, and we had a great final two hours.

Boldness, in this case, was asking the question. If my golfing friend had responded with openness and curiosity, not to press in as far as I could would have been timid. But he showed no openness, so it would have been pushy to keep going. When he said, "I am not into that," if I had responded, "Well, are you sure? Let me tell you my testimony. I used to be like . . . " I would have been getting pushy. It was appropriate at that moment to shut down the spiritual conversation and move on to another topic.

Although it may be disappointing not to get further, we should be satisfied with a seed planted, and trust God to bring the subject up again with the person. We did our job and were faithful. Now we wait on God.

Patience Versus Timidity

When having spiritual conversations we have to be as bold as possible, but also as patient as we need to be. Our posture has to be one of faithful expectation that God will give us an "Ethiopian moment" in which we will boldly proceed forward and lead someone to faith. Most Christians do the opposite. We expect the moment to be weird, the person to be upset and we will come across as pushy.

> **When having spiritual conversations, we have to be as bold as possible, but also as patient as we need to be.**

Philip knew that God had sent him, so he looked for an opportunity. He saw the man in the chariot and overheard him reading. His discernment kicked in and he asked a tension-cutting question. It took a lot of boldness from Philip to break the ice, ask the question and get into the chariot. But it also took a very open, seeking person on the other end.

The two women leaders that I spoke of in chapter ten were timid. They were scared of being pushy and allowed it to keep them from asking Jenny to make a decision for Christ. Being patient, however, is discerning when the moment is closed, and we need to wait until another time.

Learning to Be Patient

It's important to remind ourselves not to feel like every moment has to be an instant conversion or it is a failure. I would never want to imply that, and I know that many relationships take time. The principles here can be used when someone is eager to come to faith or in a slow-moving scenario.

The following discussion explains how I have learned to be patient yet bold.

Patience is one of the biggest lessons I had to learn over the last ten years. I lean toward pushiness, obviously, so I had to learn to be okay with not having each conversation be a spiritual one.[1] Today, Mom would say that I am much more enjoyable to be around and that I can talk about many things besides God.

When I took Jesus' words in John 6:44 to heart, it changed my view of sharing my faith: "No one can come to me unless the Father who sent me draws them, and I will raise them up at the last day." It is the heavenly Father's responsibility to draw people to Jesus, not mine. I am responsible to share my faith, ask questions, gauge interest and make myself available as a witness. I am responsible to be as bold as the moment requires. But I am not responsible to make anyone a Christian or force a conversation on anyone. God is sovereignly drawing people to himself, and part of that requires witnesses to help seekers interpret what it means to follow. But we are not responsible to force anything.

Two Options While We're Being Patient

When I lived at the beach right after college and before I was married, I had some crazy neighbors. I loved these guys, but they were nuts. They had six TVs in their living room so they could simultaneously watch every football game scheduled. I enjoyed watching the games with them on Sundays. But sometimes when I would walk in, they would have porn on every TV. I would walk right out. They partied hard, did drugs, watched porn, gambled a lot and lived next door to me.

These guys knew I was a Christian because I told them. I tried to get into spiritual conversations with them, but they didn't want that, and I could tell they were going to be annoyed with me if I kept bringing it up. Instead, I committed to the following.

1. Presence. Many times when we don't get results with people right away, we stop hanging out with them and move on. I committed to being present, keeping my mouth shut about Jesus and asking God to draw them to Jesus. I played volleyball with them, watched football, played cards and hung out with them as much as

I could. But I never brought up Jesus. Instead, I prayed they would develop the curiosity to raise spiritual questions, and vowed that I would respond with boldness when that time came.

We were playing poker one night when one of the guys asked me a deep spiritual question. I said, "Dude, we are in the middle of the game, let's talk later." He was surprised I didn't jump on it right there, so I explained to him that we should play the game or talk, but doing both would be hard.

Later that night, after a few of the guys had plenty to drink, another one of them started heckling me, "Beau, it's so annoying how you always bring up Jesus and make us feel bad for not following your religion."

Immediately, the guy who had asked me the question during poker said, "Shut up. Beau never brings it up. In fact, we always are the ones asking him questions, and he responds to us." I started laughing at my ironic defender, but I was also laughing inside. Being present and being willing to be bold had created this cool way for me to witness that wasn't forced. Heck, I had one of them backing me up now!

The following are a few ways a pushy person can grow in patience.

Commit to not bringing up Jesus in conversation. Since your friends and family already know where you stand, your presence will remind them every time you are with them. They will bring it up when they are ready. Then respond.

Spend more time with people. Pushy people often are agenda driven and not people driven. They move on quickly if their agenda is not working. Commit to spending a lot of time developing relationship and enjoying the people around you.

Ask your friends for feedback. Ask two or three people in your life what they honestly think about the way you carry yourself. Listen to them without being defensive, and then put into practice what they say. I stopped being pushy by having constant feedback from people who would help me grow in awareness. Many times pushy people won't ask friends for this and write off more-patient people as not bold. That is dangerous.

2. Proclamation. Spending time with people is not good enough if you are not prepared to proclaim Jesus at the right moment. I was willing to talk to my neighbors but had purposefully muzzled myself so I could increase my ability to be present with them without an agenda.

But if you are spending time with people and are not open, willing or looking for opportunities to share Jesus, you have an agenda too. Your agenda is to remain safe and comfortable, which is not so different from the pushy person's agenda. The pushy person doesn't want to let God be in control by slowing down, and you too may be maintaining control by not letting God lead you into the moment, albeit an awkward one.

The famous line "Preach the gospel always, and use words when necessary" is an awfully incomplete statement. Should you share the gospel via your actions? Absolutely. But to think that we can act our way into helping people follow Jesus is ridiculous. Our actions for Christ are signs to people at best. We can hope that people around us will become curious about why we behave a certain way, but there is no such thing as a self-interpreting sign. If we don't interpret for them with words, what the heck are they understanding? The apostle Peter admonished, "Always be prepared to give an answer to everyone who asks you to give the reason for the hope that you have. But do this with gentleness and respect" (1 Peter 3:15).

The last thing the Ethiopian needed in Acts 8 was for Philip to be present and "show him" the gospel by Philip's behavior. The Ethiopian was curious, confused and needed the Scripture to be interpreted with words. Philip knew how to proclaim Jesus from the Scripture and lead the Ethiopian to the Lord with his words. We need to be both present to seekers and willing to proclaim the words of life to them. We have to embrace both postures.

> **We need to be both present to seekers and willing to proclaim the words of life to them.**

You may be timid. You may have no problem with presence, but proclaiming Jesus is difficult for you. Start to look for and lean into moments when others are open, and realize that when someone is open, you are being bold, not pushy, as you move forward. Paul's word to you is the same he gave to Timothy: "For this reason I remind you to fan into flame the gift of God. . . . For the Spirit God gave us does not make us timid, but gives us power, love and self-discipline" (2 Timothy 1:6-7). The following are few ways a timid person can grow in boldness.

Analyze your approach. Ask yourself, *Have I ever brought up the topic of Jesus with my friends? Or do I just wait until they do?* When timid people risk bringing up Jesus in relationships, usually people are more ready than the timid realize. Timid people tend to have more relational capital than pushy people, so the time is often right to mention Jesus.

Gauge curiosity. Commit to asking your friends spiritual questions on a regular basis to gauge their curiosity. Pick two or three questions you like and start asking them as you get to know people. Remember, gauging curiosity is not pushy, it is bold.

Ask a bolder friend to help you. Ask a bolder Christian friend what he or she would do differently about a relationship you have with someone not committed to Jesus. Just as the small group leaders thought that Jenny wasn't ready for Jesus, you may be thinking the same thing about your friend. A bolder person may be able to help you see an opening you're overlooking.

Key Step: Gauge Curiosity

This week, pick one person to ask a question in order to gauge his or her curiosity about Jesus.

Reflection Questions

1. In your own words, describe the difference between being bold and being pushy.

2. What do you admire about Philip's boldness?

3. How would you describe the difference between patience and timidity?

4. Do you tend to use actions (presence) more than words (proclamation) or vice versa? How can you grow in the one not as strong?

5. In what relationship do you need to be bolder? In what relationship do you need to be more patient?

A WITNESS AT WORK

Down the Business Road

Steve Sitton, former president of AT&T (Southeast Region)

Steve Sitton has worked for three large corporations since college. He's been an officer in two of these corporations for over twenty years. As he advanced in his career, he found himself speaking to ever-larger groups of people, from two or three in the beginning to, ultimately, many thousands at a time. "I never worried about letting folks know I attend church or that I believe in God," he says. "I always liked to tell stories to make my business points, and I often would use examples of something that happened to me while singing in or growing up attending church."

As Steve became more successful in his career, he was called on to mentor others. This led to many conversations and one-on-one opportunities to talk about priorities in an advancing career. Through mistakes of his own, he was able to get his own priorities in order, and subsequently encouraged mentees to do the same: "God, family, and AT&T." "We need to stand up even more today for our faith in God, especially in the business world."

Steve often gets in conversations with nonbelievers, Muslims, Buddhists, you name it—he is always quick to say that he believes in Jesus Christ. He has never been called down for it, and he continues to look for avenues to have discussion.

"People want leadership, and they are hungry for leadership that is well grounded in faith," he says. "I freely admit that I often left my statements a little vague, but those statements have led to some very meaningful conversations."

12

How to Turn the
Conversation to Jesus

I AM NOW GOING TO WALK YOU THROUGH six crucial steps that are needed to turn casual conversations into eternal encounters. This is what I teach at the end of my seminars. To inspire you as we get started, see figure 12.1, which is an awesome tweet I got a few years back after a seminar.

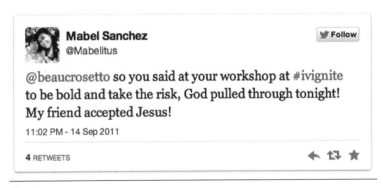

Mabel Sanchez
@Mabelitus

🐦 Follow

@beaucrosetto so you said at your workshop at #ivignite to be bold and take the risk, God pulled through tonight! My friend accepted Jesus!

11:02 PM - 14 Sep 2011

4 RETWEETS

Fig. 12.1

Embrace the Proper Mindset

No matter how well you are trained or what evangelistic tools you have in hand, you won't do much if you don't have the proper mindset about the world and being a witness. A proper mindset is 80 percent of the battle, and the right tools are 20 percent.

I was a Division I college golfer, so people often ask me for lessons. They come to me excited that I will fix their swing or help them drive the ball long and straight. But first I work on their grip, stance and posture—really boring stuff. Many people get frustrated and want to work on their swing, but I always say, "If you have a proper grip, stance and posture, then your swing will stay on track and actually do what it is supposed to do. If I work on your swing without addressing your foundation, it won't matter in the end. It will all be off track."

Teaching you how-to techniques for sharing your faith without addressing your mindset is like teaching you how to swing a golf club without giving you the proper grip and stance. Everything will be off. So with that, the following are the top three things you need to believe as you start out in witness.

1. The harvest is plentiful but the workers are few. It amazes me how many Christians do not believe "the harvest is plentiful, but the workers are few" (Luke 10:2). Most Christians I talk to believe that the harvest is small and the workers are many. This happens for a few reasons. First, they are in a heavily Christian environment, so they see more Christians than not. Maybe they go to a big church, are in a small group of all Christians or only talk about the faith with people already in the faith. Second, they aren't seeing people come to faith around them and are not in spiritual conversations with people who don't know Jesus. Many Christians talk about faith with people in church or in their small group. They don't mention their faith at work or school or with their neighbors. This contributes to believing that the harvest is small and there are plenty of workers. We often say to ourselves, *There are lots of churches and pastors to help people.* Because of this seed of bad thinking, we remove ourselves from working the harvest.

Every believer needs to step into the mission of God. We need empowered believers outside of the walls of the local church having discussions with our coworkers at

Most Christians I talk to believe that the harvest is small and the workers are many.

happy hour after work, discussing everyday life with our neighbors and so forth. If we are not careful, we cocoon ourselves in the Christian environment and start to believe that the harvest is small and the workers are many.

But when you embrace what Jesus says in Luke 10, you will begin to see the world, the office, the lecture halls and your neighborhood as filled with people needing to be harvested. And it will change the way you act.

2. You are the person God will send. When you see that God is sending you to lead others to faith, you'll walk out your door each morning knowing God is calling you, not your friend or your pastor, to reach your neighbors, your coworkers and your peers. When you take seriously the reality that God has people for you to reach in your spheres of influence, you will start to pray, train and act differently. You will feel the spiritual responsibility that Jesus placed on us.

All authority in heaven and on earth has been given to me. Therefore go and make disciples of all nations, baptizing them in the name of the Father and of the Son and of the Holy Spirit, and teaching them to obey everything I have commanded you. And surely I am with you always, to the very end of the age. (Matthew 28:18-20)

3. God will create the opportunities for you to share. The first two principles of this new mindset add some pressure, but the third principle should take the pressure off: God will create the opportunities for you to share.

You don't need to be anxious or try to force people to convert. Seekers are everywhere. You will run into them if you are looking.

Then it will be your responsibility to lead *some* of them to Jesus. But the Spirit is your guide. He will lead you and create the opportunities. You simply need to be ready to engage in conversation and relationship as he directs.

Key Step: Pray

Spend five minutes each day this week praying through these three points and getting your mindset right before you leave the house. Start your day with correct thinking and see how God changes what you encounter.[1]

Reflection Questions

1. What excites you about the evangelistic mindset?

2. List as many reasons as you can that cause you to think God will (or should) call and send someone else. Then write a truth to combat each of these blocks.

Asking Good Questions

The best people I know at getting into conversations are people who know how to ask good questions. This goes for casual conversations and spiritual ones as well.

Philip does this well in Acts 8. He first interjected with a question once he overheard the Ethiopian reading aloud. He asked the Ethiopian, "Do you understand what you are reading?" (v. 30). This question was a segue into conversation. If Philip hadn't asked the question, he probably wouldn't have gotten any further. Jesus also did this brilliantly with the woman at the well (John 4). He asked her for a drink of water, which led into a full conversation about spiritual water, and eventually allowed Jesus to reveal that he is the Messiah. The simple question, "Will you give me a drink?" was all it took.

Your job as a witness is to test people's openness to see if God is moving in them and if they are receptive and curious. Remember, I am not promoting pushiness, which is barging forward in conversation even if someone isn't open. I'm urging you to be bold where there is openness. But how can you tell when someone is open if you don't test it? You have to gauge people's interest in Jesus, and asking great questions is the best way to do that.

I always ask questions and strike up conversations with people. But with texting, instant messaging, Facebook and Twitter, many people (especially young people) do not know how to carry on a good conversation. If you're one of them, I would suggest you think of a handful of questions you can ask people when you meet them. (You can find a list of my favorite questions in appendix three.)

Your job as a witness is to test people's openness.

In a great conversation, deep things often come up. When personal issues arise or someone shares struggle, it's important to be careful and love them. Many of us are quick to jump in and give advice, which can shut down the conversation or come off as preachy, intimidating and unloving. Some of us don't know how to keep a conversation going, and we don't know how to take it deeper. Sure, some people won't want to talk further about the issue at hand, but some will.

Our job as a witness is to help people open up and get to know them better. Here's one example of how to do that by asking five good questions:

You	How are you doing today?
Friend	I am feeling kind of anxious these days.
You	Why do you think that is?
Friend	I'm not sure. I guess I feel like I am not measuring up at work.

You   I am sorry to hear that. What is going on at work?

Friend   Well, my boss called me into her office the other day and said that we are behind on the company goals and I had better hit higher numbers.

You   That's hard. Do you think your boss is being unfair? Or is it just a hard situation that has to be met? I am wondering if the anxiety is coming from her unfair expectations or the reality of the difficult situation.

Friend   I think my boss is being fair. It's just that I am doing all I can and the numbers are what they are. I have been a good performer for many years, and this year I am just not hitting the goals. I don't know what else to do.

You   That is frustrating. What do you usually do when you get stressed out? When you feel like you're at the end of your rope? What helps you cope?

Friend   I usually go home, have a glass of wine and watch a good movie to try to take my mind off things.

You   I know this might be weird, Julie, but have you ever considered how God may be able to help you find peace in frustrating circumstances? I mean, I get stressed out too, and some things like your work situation don't pan out, even though we give it our best. What if God wanted to show you more of his purpose or how he looks at your situation? What if he could give you real peace? Would you ever want to talk about that?

This last question is an example of "finding the handle," which we will talk about in the next section. It's the question you ask that turns the conversation to spiritual things. It's done in a relational way that builds on the conversation.

True, your friend could say she doesn't want to talk about what God has to do with her tough situation, and it could be awkward. But she could say yes and feel totally relieved that she has you to talk to and moved that you care about her.

Even if your friend said, "No, I don't really want to talk about that," it's likely she would still be thankful you listened to her and helped her process the situation. She will see that your faith is authentic and will respect you for that. And she will know you care about her.

The worst thing that could happen in this moment is awkwardness. The best thing, though, would be a stimulating conversation about Jesus and how he can lead people to peace.

The most socially confident people aren't afraid of awkwardness. They know it's part of relationships, especially when getting to know someone. So instead of avoiding it, they recognize it and look for ways to defuse it. One way I try to get comfortable with awkward situations is by naming them. In my mock conversation, I started to turn the conversation with "I know this may be weird." Naming the potentially uncomfortable moment may set you and the other person at ease. It gives the person permission to say, "Yes, that is weird, and I don't want to talk about it," or "No, that isn't weird. I have been thinking about that a lot lately." The person may acknowledge that it is kind of uncomfortable but is okay with moving forward. Either way, embracing the reality that awkwardness comes up in relationship, and being willing to name it in helpful ways, can set up a great conversation.

> The most socially confident people aren't afraid of awkwardness. They know it's part of relationships, especially when getting to know someone.

How to ask good questions. You may be wondering, *How do*

you go about asking questions, Beau, in everyday conversations?
My top three suggestions for becoming good at asking questions
and getting into great conversations are as follows.

1. Be genuinely curious. The people I know that are best at
asking questions love people and getting to know them. They are
curious and want to know more about people they encounter. I
have been told many times that I am curious, and what makes me
a good witness is that I love getting to know people and finding
ways to connect. This is important because we build trust with
people by letting them know we care about them. Asking great
questions is not just a gimmick to get people to convert to Jesus.
Asking questions leads to knowing people better and figuring out
how to love and serve them well. Of course when the time is right,
you will bring up Jesus. But being curious about people and
learning about them is a loving thing to do. Ask God to give you
more curiosity if you lack it.

2. Ask open-ended questions. On a more practical note, open-
ended questions are the best. Avoid asking people questions they
can answer with one word, yes or no, because this doesn't encourage them to open up. Try to ask a number of open-ended questions in a row. Be curious about them and follow the trail they take.

For example, in conversation with one of my neighbors one
night, I asked him more about his family. The conversation went
something like this.

Beau	George, tell me more about your family.
George	I have three daughters and of course my wife. All three of my daughters are still at home.
Beau	What kind of things do you like to do as a family?
George	Well, we don't do that much as a family right now.

Beau	Oh, why not? I don't mean to be insensitive, but is something going on?
George	Well, yeah. It's kind of hard to talk about, but my wife and I are having some trouble.
Beau	George, I am sorry to hear that. If you want to talk more, please let me know. I don't want to assume you want to talk about it, but if you want to, I am all ears.
George	Well, I guess it would be good to vent a little bit. She is having an affair, and I know it. But she won't admit it.

Obviously this turned into a pretty sad conversation, but you can see from this example that just being curious about my neighbor and asking him a few open-ended questions allowed this conversation to happen. I didn't start the night in my man cave with the agenda to get into his marriage problems. But God took it there, and I was able to listen to him well, talk to him about God's perspective and pray for him. It has become a good relationship. He appreciates me listening and helping him interpret all that is going on.

3. Affirm the person, then ask another question. When you ask someone an open-ended question, affirm the person's answer and then ask another question that opens him or her up further about what was said. This is important. Nobody wants to be asked leading questions; they want to be asked about what they said and feel as though you are listening. For example, ask about the person's favorite hobby. Affirm the person and then ask a further question about that specific hobby (for example, How often do you do it? When do you do it? What excites you about that hobby?).

Key Step: Have a Conversation

Strike up a conversation this week and see how long you can talk to the person about him- or herself. Try asking as many open-ended questions as you can.

Reflection Questions

1. List several good questions you can use in everyday conversations. What are your favorites?

2. How comfortable are you at keeping a conversation going? Do you enjoy getting to know people in deeper ways?

Finding the Handle

Ben and I had a twenty-minute ride on our way to volleyball, which gave us plenty of time to talk. As we were cruising down Crenshaw Boulevard with the windows down and Led Zeppelin cranking, he turned the volume down a bit and told me he was struggling at work. I was caught off-guard by his vulnerability, but I continued to listen and ask questions. He brought up a ton of feelings about his boss, his current position and his worries that, after thirty years at this company, he wasn't sure they were going the right way. He was angry and confused. I didn't offer him any advice. I continued to listen, ask more questions and offer the occasional, "Man, that sucks. I'm sorry."

We got to the volleyball court and the game was intense. The group that plays in our league is crazy: highly competitive people and unclear out-of-bounds lines equals lots of conflict. But Ben loves going there, and because I was a pretty good player, I could take the yelling, arguing and smack talk. I kept going back each week, the players started calling me "the Priest," and Ben and I got more chances to connect.

My relationship with Ben grew, and he continued to process his work and life anxieties with me. The fourth time we went to play volleyball, I sensed from God that it was time for me to bring up Jesus. Ben had let me into a number of things in his life, and I could see some handles that I could grab and turn to open various doors to conversation about Jesus. I didn't want to pressure him about faith, but I did want to see if he was open. We had trust, but I was still nervous.

We were at a stoplight and my heart raced when I asked, "Ben, I know this is weird, but have you ever considered where God may be in all of this?"

"Not really," he replied.

Sensing he needed a little more clarity, I jumped back in.

"Well, you know I am a Christian, and I know that God can help you with your anger and your anxieties. I would love to explain how that would be possible, if you want to know it."

He responded quickly, "I do want to know about God. I mean, I do believe he is out there somewhere, and I am sure he has some plan. But I don't know what that means at all. Beau, I need you to explain to me heaven and hell and where we go when we die. I am scared of dying. I need to know how all this stuff works."

Wow, I was pleasantly shocked. Because we were almost at our game, I couldn't fully launch into the gospel, so I responded to him pretty simply. "Yeah, man, I would love to talk to you about those things. Heaven is real, and you can go there. But God is also very concerned with helping you live fully now too. Let's grab a burger soon and talk about this. As far as right now is concerned, you need to know that God is real, he does love you, and he can work in your life. He wants to reveal himself to you, and I can help you."

Ben took a deep sigh of relief and sincerely thanked me. I could tell he felt cared for, and I could see how much these things were weighing on his mind. Though our conversations continued during car ride after car ride for the rest of the season, for a while Ben did not respond to meeting with me for that burger.

Start where the person is. Having the right mindset, listening well and asking great questions can help you capture a moment and not let it pass by. But once you have someone's attention and Jesus comes up, you have to start right where he or she is. As Acts 8:35 tells us so aptly, "Then Philip began with that very passage of Scripture and told him the good news about Jesus."

Philip didn't come out of left field with a gospel diagram and start sharing things that made no sense to the Ethiopian. He entered into the Isaiah passage the Ethiopian had been reading and built the conversation from there.

Jesus was a master at this too. He talked with the woman at the well about water, with the fishermen about fishing, with the adulterous woman about her accusers and so on. Jesus knew how to engage people where they were and turn the conversation from that point.

One major reason some have difficulty sharing their faith is that they have a negative image of a faith conversation. Perhaps it's someone pushing a tract into another's hand, explaining that the person is a sinner who must repent or go to hell, and then offering the gift of salvation in Jesus. These methods worked at some point, but I don't see them working very well today, at least in my context. That isn't a caring or helpful approach.

If people are not burdened by sin, it will do no good to say they are sinners going to hell. It doesn't connect. While there is a significant reason for bringing up the reality of sin and hell, it is a horrible starting place with someone who has not asked you about it. Unfortunately, this is the primary image most of us have when we hear we should "share the gospel."

This image is reinforced by being told we should *always* start by asking people questions like, "Do you know where you will go if you died today?" "Do you acknowledge you are a sinner?" or "Did you know the wages of sin is death?" These are all true, but imagine how damaging it might have been if I launched straight in from that angle with Ben.

You shouldn't use a script that feels inauthentic and will cause your friends to tune you out. Unfortunately, your friends who grew up in America likely have the same negative image of an evangelist that you do.

Your friends who grew up in America likely have the same negative image of an evangelist that you do.

When we look at the witness of Jesus and Philip, we see that it is best to start where the person is. Let's learn to share the good news of Jesus from where our friends are currently standing. That is why it is important to listen well and ask good questions.

Figure 12.2 is another continuum to help you think about how to approach sharing the faith with someone.

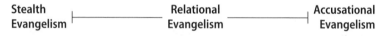

| Stealth Evangelism | | Relational Evangelism | | Accusational Evangelism |

Fig. 12.2. Evangelism continuum

Here's how I define the terms. *Stealth evangelism* is attentive to where someone is spiritually but never starting a conversation. *Accusational evangelism* uses a gospel presentation that starts without concern for where the person is spiritually. *Relational evangelism* is an act of love that syncs the gospel to the current reality of the person.

Obviously we want to be great relational evangelists, which means starting with concern for the other person. It is important to note that relational evangelism does not mean we have a formal relationship with the person. We may have just met the person and quickly got into a spiritual conversation. But starting where the person is—being relational—is always the best.

Door of awkwardness. Ben needed me to start with his anger and anxieties, and talk with him about what God has to do with those things. I was able to do that by finding handles in Ben's story. Finding handles is so important in order to have spiritual conversations with people. *A handle is a theme or struggle in a person's life* *that emerges in conversation.* As people share their lives, common themes, struggles and joys will emerge that you can grab onto and begin to turn the conversation and introduce Jesus.

As I bring you into my story with Ben, you can see the handles that emerged.

- *I am frustrated at work, and I don't like my boss.*
- *I am feeling a lot of anxiety in life.*
- *I struggle with anger and have since I was a kid.*

I picture the witnessing encounter to look a lot like myself and Ben standing on one side of a door, while on the other side is a divine encounter waiting to happen. The issues and concerns presenting themselves in the conversation are the handle of that invisible door in your conversation. That door represents the barrier between your friend and the divine encounter waiting to happen. Someone needs to turn the handle and open the door. This is the job of the witness, and the loving way to turn the handle is by starting where the nonbeliever is, engaging a question or concern and turning the conversation toward Jesus (see fig. 12.3).

Fig. 12.3. The barrier between your friend and a divine encounter. Art by Juliano Yi.

The way to relationally and gently open a door for a conversation about Jesus is by grabbing and turning handles like frustration, anxiety and anger. This is the loving thing to do. After I was able to build trust with Ben, and he freely shared his struggles with me, I did the loving thing and grabbed onto these handles and talked to him further about them. Because I believe Jesus is the absolute best thing for Ben, the one who can heal him and help him live as he was meant to live, I want to introduce him to Ben. But if I mentioned Jesus out of the blue and with a scripted message, it would feel awkward and would not serve Ben. I want to show Ben that Jesus is right behind the barriers he is presenting.

We need to know how to grab handles and turn a conversation toward Jesus. We need to be able to speak about Jesus' relevance to issues like anxiety, anger and frustration. How do we do this well? Through telling Jesus' stories in the Bible and our own transformation stories. You'll see how I did that with Ben in the next section.

What happens when there is no handle? When I can't find a handle in the conversation, I keep asking questions. If the conversation is coming to a close, I will make an effort to get together again with the person and keep learning about him or her. I am willing to be bold and turn the conversation to Jesus, but not until I know enough about the person to lovingly and relationally turn the conversation through a handle offered me.

Key Step: Relax

The gospel is not a cookie-cutter formula, so you can relax. Don't be in a hurry. Take your time getting to know people around you and find the handles in their lives. When you have some handles, which may happen faster than you expect, look for ways to turn your conversations to Jesus. But don't rush the conversations until you have some handles.

Reflection Questions

1. Where would you have taken the conversation with Ben?

2. What do you like about finding handles?

3. Ask God to show you some handles in conversations you have had recently. How could you do what I did with Ben?

Sharing Your Story

My wife and I got into a significant fight one night and needed help from our friends to sort it out and reconcile. I had gotten angry with her and lost my temper. For good reason, she was upset with me. We fully worked it out with our friends, said our apologies, forgave each other and learned how we can love each other better going forward.

As I was praying after the fight, God brought Ben to mind and told me I needed to tell him about my fight with my wife and how I struggle with anger too. I also needed to tell Ben how I work through fights like these with Jesus' help, seeking transformation by submitting my life to God and his leading.

As Ben and I were driving to volleyball the next weekend, I told Ben that I had gotten in a bad fight with my wife earlier in the week and lost my temper. I told him how I struggle with anger and that I am asking God to transform me. I told him that, as a Christian, when I make mistakes and sin, I confess my sin to God and ask him to forgive me. I also ask God to fill me with more of his love so I can live as I was meant to live.

Ben was intrigued, but also quick to tell me that I shouldn't worry about it. After all, everyone makes mistakes.

But I had a different take. "Ben, being a Christian means you believe God is real and present, and has relationship with us. It means that I no longer guide my own life. I now follow Jesus and ask him to transform me into the loving person we see he is in Scripture.

This is what I want to talk to you about. God can help you with your anger too if you want to give him control of your life. He can change you and transform you. You don't have to stay the same."

Ben thanked me, and again said we needed to talk more later. He said he wanted to go out for a drink and hash this out. He did want to learn about God.

The power of lordship stories. Story is important in sharing faith and turning casual conversations to eternal ones. Sharing our transformational stories, especially those that show how we submit our life to

> **When we share our brokenness and allow others to see our emotional junk, they also can see how we are letting Jesus change us.**

Jesus as Lord, allows us to be vulnerable and relate to our friends. When we share our brokenness and allow others to see our emotional junk, they also can see how we are letting Jesus change us. It shows them that we are normal human beings no different than they are. We are not holier than thou, and we too have real problems. It also reveals that Jesus is real and that transformation is possible.

When we do this, people start to see how they can be changed. It allows them to reflect on how they could be different with Jesus in their life. Without having to look at themselves, they can observe our lives, see our brokenness and evaluate whether that could work for them. They don't need an argument about Christ's divinity and resurrection; they need to see Christ is real and can transform lives. Showing them how Jesus is transforming us trumps any argument. Our job in this experience-based culture is to show people that Jesus works and changes us. They usually don't need to debate the resurrection or the divine nature. We first must show them what a real and vibrant relationship with Christ looks like.

Know a few stories well. If you are going to lead an open life in front of others and allow them to see how Jesus is transforming you, you should know how to tell a few of your own transformation stories as well as God's story.

Your friends will have a variety of areas that need transformation, and you'll want to be able to share with them your experiences in those areas. You'll also meet new people, and you'll need to find handles in conversation with them in order to share how Christ has transformed your life.

Listening well can help you find the handle to crack the door, and knowing how to tell the right story can kick the door wide open.

> **Vulnerability begets vulnerability. As your sharing matches the person's openness, the conversation can go to much deeper spiritual places.**

Connected to the handle on the front of the door are the person's issues and concerns (see fig. 12.3). These become visible as you ask questions and listen well. But as you turn the conversation toward Jesus and begin to open the door, you start to uncover deeper questions, vulnerabilities and stories. Picture yourself with story in one hand and Scripture in the other (see fig. 12.4). As the door cracks, you want to find the right story in your life to match the person's story behind the door. Learning

Fig. 12.4. The door begins to open. Art by Juliano Yi.

to connect in this way often drives the conversation further. In a sense vulnerability begets vulnerability. As your sharing matches the person's openness, the conversation can go to much deeper spiritual places. You are helping this person to open wide and become aware of his or her vulnerabilities. Then you can help the person see how Jesus can overcome those problems in a powerful way.

Another reason that I always have a few transformational stories ready to share is that it helps me with my own discipleship. We cannot thrive evangelistically on our initial conversion moment testimony in every situation. We need to have stories of continual transformation. Though I share my story of coming to faith in Christ frequently, I also try to share the most relevant story of how God is currently working in my life. If we are truly following Jesus, we need to allow him to regularly confront us in our sin, submit to his changes, correct our course and move forward. It's helpful to share this process with people who don't know Jesus.

I have learned how to share quick snapshots of transformation in my life—stories of transformation from anger to love, from lust to intimacy, from anxiety to peace and so on. These take one to two minutes to tell.[2] I am prepared at any moment to share how God has changed me and is changing me in these areas. I want people to see a vibrant, dynamic and real relationship with Jesus in my life. I want them to see how going to Jesus for change, comfort or renewal works, even if it is not perfect.

Key Step: Write It Out

List four or five transformational stories from your life that you could tell. Pick one and write it out. See appendix four for a worksheet to help you.

Reflection Questions

1. Think of an interpersonal conflict you have worked through with someone. How can you tell that story to a friend like Ben?

2. Ask the Spirit if there's someone ready who should hear the transformational story you wrote in the "Key Step."

Sharing the Gospel

Ben and I have been playing volleyball together for over a year now, and we have had many car rides to and from our games. Though we talk deeply about life and Jesus on those twenty-minute drives, we still have not gone out to talk over burgers and fries. It is incredible that we are so connected; yet he is avoiding "the talk" at the same time. Even more odd is that nearly every week Ben comes to my driveway while I am playing with the kids and says, "We need to have the talk, man." I always tell him, "Ben, you know I am available. Let's do it. I have the time."

Every conversation leads to the time we actually have "the talk." When the time comes, how will I simply yet powerfully share the gospel with Ben? Here are a few ways I do it with others.

Leading to the Jesus story. I typically try to frame a conversation around a biblical passage in which Jesus interacts with another person. It's a way of embedding our conversation in a story that the seeker can look at in the Bible.

If Ben sits down with me for a meal or comes over to my man cave for a chat, I will do everything I can to crack open the Bible and show him a powerful encounter between Jesus and seeker. In my experience this always leads to the best moments. And if Ben is still confused or wants to know more about what we talked about, he can go back to that story and soak in it.

Whenever I can get a person into *a Jesus story*, it makes it that much easier for me to share *the Jesus story* with them. A Jesus story is any story in the Gospels where Jesus interacts with someone. *The* Jesus story is the work of his life, death, resurrection and return. It's the message of salvation for humanity and the world.

Of course this means I have to know how to tell Jesus stories well. Just as I need a handful of transformation stories about my own life, I also want to know how to tell at least five Jesus stories, so I can look at them with a seeker right on the spot.

The following are the top five Jesus stories that I talk through with people.

1. The prodigal son (Luke 15:11-32). Even if we turn our back on God and act like he is dead, God will be waiting for us when we turn back to him. This passage shows the seeker that Jesus waits to pour out his love and forgiveness on us even though we don't deserve it.

2. Jesus turns water into wine (John 2:1-11). Jesus turns 180 gallons of water into wine! That is eleven kegs! People may say that religion is boring, but Jesus' first miracle proves that wrong. This passage shows the seeker how this miracle foreshadowed the extravagant love and forgiveness Jesus poured out on the cross.

3. The adulterous woman (John 8:1-11). A seeker who has sinned in a horrible way may have many accusers. But Jesus is at the seeker's side, and he doesn't condemn the person. This passage shows the seeker that Jesus is ready to forgive and say what he said to the adulterous woman, "Go now and leave your life of sin."

4. The calling of Levi (Luke 5:27-32). Jesus calls the worst of sinners to follow him. Not only did he call Levi to follow, he had dinner at Levi's house with all of his sinful friends. This passage shows the seeker that Jesus does not call perfect people to follow him.

5. The seven woes (Matthew 23:13-29). No one likes hypocrites, including Jesus. In this passage Jesus gives religious hypocrites an earful. This passage shows the seeker that if they are fed up with hypocrisy in the church, Jesus is more on their side than they think.

Pick five of your favorite stories in the Gospels, study them and figure out how to communicate them well with seekers. Jesus stories are powerful; they open our friends' eyes to see who Jesus is. These stories aren't dogmatic and aren't propositional truths. People can find themselves in the stories, which is important and helpful in today's culture.

Going back to the door of awkwardness (see fig. 12.4), in one hand you, the witness, are holding the power of Scripture, and your job is to know and share Scripture to open conversations further. Great questions and personal stories work well to crack doors open, but seekers need Jesus, and you need to know how to match the right Bible story with the seeker's story.[3]

Though I sometimes share Scriptures from the epistles, I don't start there. I start with Jesus in order to help people see their own story within the Bible story, hoping they eventually see their story within God's story. I want to help people see Jesus firsthand in Scripture to awaken them to God himself.

Components of the gospel. Once I turn the conversation to Jesus with a Jesus story, there are a few ways the dialogue can go. Again, it's not about script but flow. Jesus didn't have a pat answer or script he used with every person. He talked with people as they needed.

Think about it: Jesus talked to the rich young ruler one way, the adulterous woman another and Zacchaeus still another. Did Jesus preach different gospels? No, he simply communicated different facets of the good news as he met people in different places of life.

> **Did Jesus preach different gospels? No, he simply communicated different facets of the good news as he met people in different places of life.**

We want to do the same with people as we encounter them in conversation. However, to communicate the good news of God well, we have to be cognizant of those parts of the gospel that are essential to the message of Jesus, Peter, Paul and the early followers.

Let me help you see the core gospel components—the four Ps—

that I zero in on when the moment is right. In a given conversation I hope to get to all of them, but I try to start right where they are.

1. Pardon. Theologically speaking, every person you meet is full of sin. But some people are especially burdened by their sin. It's at the forefront of their thinking, it's carried in their emotions and they have a real conviction about their mistakes. With people like this, you can start with the reality that God pardons us and offers us 100 percent forgiveness on the cross. "Therefore, if anyone is in Christ, the new creation has come: The old has gone, the new is here!" (2 Corinthians 5:17).

The good news is that we can be new creations. Jesus has come to make us new and we can start over free of charge. We can be renewed, remade and completely forgiven. We do not have to carry any guilt or shame from what we have done or who we have been.

It is imperative you explain the cross well. Without the cross, there is nothing. The goal of a gospel conversation is to get your friend to the cross of Christ. The cross is the fulcrum by which everything is changed. The cross and our understanding of what Jesus did there makes available our relationship to the Father in heaven and to his kingdom. Jesus died on the cross for the sin in the world (personal as well as systemic sin) and buried it in the grave. It is hidden forever out of our sight.

We have to explain the cross to people so they can see who makes all this possible. The new personal and corporate realities of the kingdom of God are only possible because Jesus died on the cross and shattered Satan's power when Jesus rose again. This *is* good news![4]

The only way anyone can have their sin paid for and be reconciled to God is through Jesus' death on the cross. Our sin separates us from God, and Jesus died on the cross to pay for our sin and bring us back into relationship with God.

2. Power. Some people you'll meet are in need of God's power. Maybe they are sick or suffering an injustice or are even possessed by demons. The good news for them is the power we find in Jesus' resurrection. This person does not need you to first present the side of God who forgives us for our personal sins. They need you to preach the victory of Christ on the cross and his resurrection from death. They need hope that things can be different. They need to hear about a victorious God in areas that are different from personal sin.[5]

In Ephesians 1:18-21, Paul says,

> I pray that the eyes of your heart may be enlightened in order that you may know . . . [God's] incomparably great power for us who believe. That power is the same as the mighty strength he exerted when he raised Christ from the dead and seated him at his right hand in the heavenly realms, far above all rule and authority, power and dominion, and every name that is invoked, not only in the present age but also in the one to come.

In this letter to the church, Paul wants us to know that we have incredible power through the indwelling of the Holy Spirit. The same power that raised Christ from the dead now lives in all believers.

When I get into conversations with people who are struggling, I preach Christ and his power. I assure them that if Jesus can raise people from the dead, then he can resolve their problem too. When we surrender our lives to Jesus, we come under a new kind of power. This power gives us what we need to live a victorious life: we can defeat sinful habits, find freedom from disease and have a new attitude on life.

Every person needs the good news that Jesus forgives them of their sin. But they also need good news that they can be in relationship with the living God, who has total power over death as well as their current situation. If they need change, go to Jesus. If they need victory, go to Jesus. If they need to be lifted up, go to Jesus. He has the power not found in this world.

The same power that raised Christ from the dead is available to all who accept Jesus into their life. The Holy Spirit, God's presence, lives in people who follow Jesus. That Spirit is full of incomparable power, and we can have access to it too!

3. *Purpose.* Other people lack meaning in their lives. They are dissatisfied and want to know if there is more to life. They are open to God because he might have a greater plan for them. With people like this, I always talk about the kingdom of God.[6]

Jesus said, "The kingdom of God has come near" (Mark 1:15). I latch onto this phrase when talking to people about Jesus because I love to explain that Jesus has a great role for us to play in his new kingdom.

Yes, Jesus died on the cross for our sins. And yes, one day we go to heaven. But what is exciting about Jesus ushering in the kingdom is that we can be different now as we too help usher in this kingdom. In *Kingdom Come* Allen Wakabayashi explains the Jewish expectation regarding the kingdom:

> They were not thinking about how to secure themselves a place in heaven after they died. The phrase "kingdom of heaven," which we find frequently in Matthew's Gospel where the others have "kingdom of God," does not refer to a place, called "heaven," where God's people will go after death. It refers to the rule of heaven, that is, of God, being brought to bear in the present world. Thy kingdom come, said Jesus, thy will be done, *on earth as in heaven.* Jesus' contemporaries knew that the creator God intended to bring justice and peace to his world here and now.[7]

When we come into relationship with Jesus and start to follow him, he flips our purpose upside down. We get a whole new paradigm with which to look at life. Jesus is determined to establish God's reign and rule on earth. Jesus is bringing into existence what is meant to be. Namely, Jesus desires right relationships between God and humans, between us and other humans, and between humans and creation. Jesus is establishing a way in which things work on earth as he intended.

> When we come into relationship with Jesus and start to follow him, he flips our purpose upside down. We get a whole new paradigm with which to look at life.

Jesus' followers are brought into a grand adventure. Our lives are directed toward others and not ourselves. Jesus teaches his followers how to find life by serving others and living a life that ushers in his rule and reign on earth. We become agents of his kingdom; we connect other people to Jesus and help them submit to his leadership. We also pray for healing, do justice and bring reconciliation to individuals and systems. Through the way we live, we lobby for the things of God to flourish on this planet.

Our purpose changes when we come into alignment with Jesus. As we follow Jesus, we think differently about our time, money, relationships and occupation. Jesus will show us how to live with purpose in his kingdom and the part we are to play in establishing the kingdom on earth.

4. Presence. Sometimes people are simply down and out, somewhat like Job. The last thing they need is a message about forgiveness, power or purpose. They need presence. They need your presence and ultimately the presence of Christ.

For some people the good news is that Jesus is with them. The starting point of the journey to Christ may very well be that he is Emmanuel—God with us. This good news initially may come simply through your presence, which eventually leads to the message of Emmanuel. Ultimately, God's presence restored Job's faith. And when Lazarus died, before Jesus said anything to Mary he simply wept and was present to her.

Some people you encounter will need presence more than anything else. This is how God will be revealed to them.

Belief. Whether a person is introduced to Jesus through pardon, power, purpose or presence, I eventually share that to become a Christian he or she has to choose to believe in Jesus and trust the things he says. Christianity is a religion of the heart. The Bible is clear that we are not saved by what we do but by who we trust. Our job as a witness is to help people believe in the life, death, resurrection and return of Jesus. A person who turns from a self-directed life and trusts in Jesus has become a Christian.

There is no one clear-cut way to share the gospel. There are many facets of the good news of God. Sharing the good news should be contextual. It's okay not to cover every component of the gospel in a conversation. In turning casual conversations into eternal ones we need to help people take the next step that gets them closer to Jesus.

> Christianity is a religion of the heart. The Bible is clear that we are not saved by what we do, but by who we trust.

Key Step: Learn a Jesus Story

Pick your favorite Jesus story and practice telling it to someone.

Reflection Questions

1. What are your five favorite Jesus stories? Why?

2. Which of the four Ps is easiest for you to talk about, and which is hardest? Imagine you need to explain the hardest one to a nonbelieving friend, and write it out in one paragraph.

Inviting a Response

The final thing you'll need to do when turning casual conversations into eternal encounters is invite a response. This is crucial. Opening a spiritual conversation without closing it by inviting the person to respond to God is like doing surgery without stitching up the wound.

> Opening a spiritual conversation without closing it by inviting the person to respond to God is like doing surgery without stitching up the wound.

Our seeking friends are not used to having conversations about God. God's Spirit is powerfully at work in them when we have those conversations—it awakens their souls, causes conviction and brings up sadness and pain—and those things weigh on them if left open. Regarding this the apostle John says,

> When he comes, he will prove the world to be in the wrong about sin and righteousness and judgment: about sin, because people do not believe in me; about righteousness, because I am going to the Father, where you can see me no longer; and about judgment, because the prince of this world now stands condemned. (John 16:8-11)

This is why we need to invite people to take a next step and respond to Jesus.

In the Gospels, every time Jesus had a significant conversation with a seeking person, he invited a response. He encouraged people to be born again, told them to go and sin no more, to follow him, to tell people about him, and much more. When Jesus got into conversations with people, he asked them to take a step of faith. Remember, we are asking people to follow a living God. He is on the move. He wants them to move too. He wants them to take a step.

But we don't always have to ask people to accept Jesus. That is not the only challenge we can give. Do I hope to soon invite Ben to start following Jesus? Yes. I absolutely hope I get to invite him to turn from himself and his life of sin, and accept Christ's forgiveness and new way of life. But, as I've done with Ben on our

> In the Gospels, every time Jesus had a significant conversation with a seeking person, he invited a response.

rides to volleyball, there are other steps I might give to people who are not quite ready. For example, I might ask them to take steps of faith with questions like:

* Can I pray for you right now?
* Would you like to go to church with me this week?
* Would you like to start meeting with me to look at Jesus' life?
* Would you like to start a relationship with Jesus today?

My go-to line. I love to be direct about my hopes for people, whether I just met them or they are longtime friends. I'll say something like this: "Hey, Joe, I know you know that I am a Christian. I want you to know that I love talking about my faith and I love helping people figure out how to have a relationship with God. You know this is important to me. I also know that many people have questions about God but don't know where to go for help. Most people who don't go to church don't have a lot of friends they can talk to about God. And it can be embarrassing to bring that up or have to break the ice. So I want you to know that if you ever want to talk about faith, I would love it. Any time. Seriously. I love helping people with their questions, and it won't be a burden to me at all. I am telling you this because I am not going to be that annoying Christian who keeps bringing it up. I am not going to bug you. But you can know that if you ever have the desire to talk, I am here for you."

Whenever I say this to someone, cool things happen. More often than not, they say something like, "Thanks, I would love that. Let's grab lunch sometime." Other times, I have had people come back to me a week later and say, "You know how you said you don't mind talking with me about God? Well, I do have a question I keep thinking about . . ." Plenty of people have not taken me up on my offer, but I know they respect me for doing it, and they see that I care.

I do this because I want to create space for spiritual conversations to happen. Your friends who are not following Jesus have questions. Many of them are embarrassed to bring up God, or they don't know how to do it. You are paying the "awkward bill" for them by bringing it up first. You are creating space for them to say, "You know what, I do have questions."

If you think you feel uncomfortable bringing this up with your friends, imagine how weird they may feel bringing it up as an outsider to faith. By letting your friends know you want to talk and that it's an open invitation, they can step in more easily as God works in their heart.

What if they say no? One of my other neighbors, Jim, had a great conversation with me one day in my backyard, and we talked about many spiritual things. We got deep into a conversation about Jesus. Then I asked him if he wanted to talk further about the Christian message at some point. He said, "No, not really." I've continued to be his friend and have him over for talks about everyday things. By doing this, I show him that our spiritual conversation wasn't abnormal or cause for us to stop hanging out.

People need to see that Christians aren't weird or don't have to shut down unless they are talking about Jesus. Our friends need to see that they are not our project. In fact, it is important to grow closer to them once we bring up the topic of faith and they reject our offer. It demonstrates more than we can imagine.

What if I don't know the answer? People often ask me what I do when I don't know the answer to questions seekers ask me. You too may be scared that you will get stumped. My response is: It's okay to be stumped! You are being authentic when you tell your friend, "I don't know the answer to that question, but I will get back to you about it."

Becky Pippert, author of *Out of the Saltshaker and into the World*, would say something similar: "I don't know the answer but can't wait to investigate it."[8] It is fine to get stuck on a point in a conversation and then get back to the person later. This shows you are vulnerable and not a know-it-all. People will appreciate this human element of your witness. If the person is truly a seeker, he or she will not mind getting the answer from you later. In fact, it will be appreciated. **What if someone is mean to me?** Some people may get hostile when you bring up your faith. It is inevitable that Jesus will strike a nerve with certain people. It is important in these moments to remember Matthew 5:11-12: "Blessed are you when people insult you, persecute you and falsely say all kinds of evil against you because of me. Rejoice and be glad, because great is your reward in heaven, for in the same way they persecuted the prophets who were before you." Though these verses are counterintuitive, God honors those who stand up for Jesus and are persecuted for their stand.

When this happens, resist the temptation to argue. Instead, be polite and move on. Assume that the reason the person is angry is not your fault, and take great joy in the fact that "great is your reward in heaven." Remember, it is not your job to twist someone's arm or to convince a hostile person. Pray for the person once you are done with the interaction and continue to love him or her.

Key Step: Identify

Identify and write your favorite way to invite a response from seekers.

Reflection Questions

1. Think of someone who invited you to respond to God at some point in your life. Thank God for him or her.

2. What is one barrier or fear you feel in inviting people to respond to Jesus?

3. Ask the Spirit to bring one person to mind and give you the opportunity to invite him or her to respond to Christ. Write out how you might do that. Then pray for an opportunity to talk with that person this week.

Epilogue

Don't Keep Them Waiting

I WILL NEVER FORGET THE **S**UNDAY that Ben drove into our joint driveway just as I was pulling in from church. With his windows rolled down and still in the car, he tilted his sunglasses and said with urgency, "Beau, we need to talk today. It's time I give my life to someone else."

As the adrenaline from excitement rushed through my body, I calmly said to him, "Absolutely, Ben. Come over tonight and we can talk in the man cave." Today was different; I could tell in his voice he was going to show up. But I couldn't help but think back on the numerous times he had stood me up before. Would he show?

At 2:30, about two hours later, he walked into my man cave and said "shut the door," and we launched into a couple hours of conversation and prayer. Ben accepted Jesus into his life and we prayed together to start this new journey.[1]

I am not sure I have the words to explain how incredible that felt. Like I said earlier in the book, the feeling of seeing a friend come to faith is so grand, it's the most peaceful sense of purpose you will ever feel—I was put on this earth to help people connect to their loving Father in heaven. What gets better than that?

Two years of investment in Ben. Long conversations, many prayers and ample amounts of love poured out—all for the hope of this moment.

Ben needed a witness. He needed someone to incarnate into his world, get to know him, love on him for those two years and speak boldly about Jesus at the right times. In his own words, he said, "I can't believe God moved you next door to me."

What about you? Whom has God moved you next door to?

I started this book with the chapter title "Someone Is Waiting for You," in which I said that all around you are people longing for a witness, whether they can articulate it or not. My dad, my sister, Yoshiko, Alan, Sam and Alex were all waiting. They needed a witness, and I stepped in. I had the opportunity to see them all come to Christ! I had the privilege of standing in the front row and watching as they experienced the choice wine. It's great fun.

You have people waiting too, and I hope you step in like I did and continue to do so. Yes, it will be tense at times and feel a bit strange. But isn't everything that makes life truly worth living a bit wild?

God will speak to you if you listen. He will lead you down interesting roads if you follow. He will give you the right words if you will speak. He will give you the courage to overcome awkward tensions if you will step out. God will do all of this because he knows people are waiting for him, and he wants to meet them.

The question is, Will you be the matchmaker that sets this whole thing up, or will you keep people waiting?

Beyond Awkward

Great matchmakers have to break the tension many times. You will have to step into the middle and say, "This relationship should happen." That can be awkward. Especially when it is about relationship with the invisible God.

But there is life beyond awkward. I am not saying that awkwardness will go away or that you won't ever again feel uncomfortable. But you can get beyond the awkwardness and fear that control your life as a witness.

Think about the time you made your first presentation at work, gave your first talk in front of a class or asked someone on a first date. Fear probably gripped you. You were undoubtedly a little awkward and not very fluid. We call it nerves or the jitters. You weren't quite yourself in those moments, and a mentor would probably say, "It's okay. You will get more comfortable as you do it more. Don't worry about it and keep going!"

Evangelism and sharing your faith can be the same way. It is not that you won't ever be scared or feel tension again. But you can choose not to let it control you. Keep following the Spirit, taking risks and stepping into God-ordained moments. You will become more comfortable. It will feel more natural, and you will become pretty good at it.

I bless you in the name of Jesus to lead many people to Christ.

How beautiful on the mountains
    are the feet of those who bring good news,
who proclaim peace,
    who bring good tidings,
    who proclaim salvation,
who say to Zion,
    "Your God reigns!" (Isaiah 52:7)

Acknowledgments

Nothing worthwhile can be done alone, and this book is no different. This book would not have been published without all the help I have received.

First, a huge thanks to my wife, Kristina, for all the verbal processing, for your great thoughts and for giving me the time and space to write.

The following people gave me in-depth feedback about the manuscript: James Choung, Rick Richardson, Beth Severson, Doug Shaupp, Tracey Gee, Ram Sridharan, Jon Ball, Matt Nault, Chris Nichols, Stephanie Teng, Tyler Allred, Dave Ferguson and Sarah Schilling. They helped shape this book by pressing me for clarity, suggesting additional chapters, informing me that certain parts weren't good even though I thought they were, and helping me stay true to my voice. They also prayed for and encouraged me along the way. I cannot thank them enough for their edits as well as amazing insights and ideas. Many of their thoughts are in this book.

Many others helped me get the book accepted and gave me incredible insights as I got started with the project. I give my heartfelt thanks to Eric, Alan, Will, Ross, Melissa, Mona, Carolyn, Yvonne, Brandt, George, James, Rob, Hayley, Gina, Pam, Jon, David, Lindsay, Matt, Ryan, Dan, Dave and Joey. Thank you, Dave Zimmerman, my editor, for mentoring me as a first-time author and showing me the ropes. You took a chance on me and helped me develop this idea from day one.

Last but not least, thanks to the team of marketers who are responsible for you even reading this book—Andrew Bronson, Deborah Gonzalez and Adrianna Wright.

Five Guidelines for Hearing God

James Choung, my good friend and the author of *True Story*, originally came up with these ideas on hearing God.[1] As James and I started a church in our neighborhood, we have fleshed out these guidelines more clearly as a community. He has graciously given me permission to share them here.

Learning to recognize Jesus' voice in everyday situations and responding to what you hear is at the center of following Jesus. No one does it perfectly, so it's important to keep practicing in community, which is where God's Spirit dwells. The following guidelines should get you started.

Scripture: What Does the Bible Say About Hearing God?

The Bereans were considered of more noble character than the Thessalonians because they tested everything Paul said against the Scriptures (Acts 17:11). Scripture study is vital: God won't contradict what he's already said. And knowing what God said and how he said it will help you recognize when and how God speaks today.

Too many people "hear God" saying things to them that are inconsistent with the Bible and have nothing to do with the character of God. If what you think you are hearing from God goes against what Scripture says, then what you have heard is not from God. Chalk up what you have heard to the bad burrito you ate for lunch.

We need to be especially careful in our culture when we talk about hearing from God. Today, most people do not believe in truth. They function as relativists—believing and doing whatever makes sense to them. But God's Scripture is the anchor for all that we believe and follow as Christians. His voice will never go against the written Word.

You are not bad if you hear something that goes against Scripture. You are human. However, it is important to realize and be humble enough to admit that what you heard was not from God. The better we know Scripture, the easier it becomes to make sure what we are thinking, hearing and desiring is in line with God.

Prayer: What Is God Saying to You About What You Heard?

God speaks to us all the time, and the expectation is that we hear his voice (John 10:2-4). When you pray, what do you hear?

It is surprising how many times we get an idea or sense God is putting something on our heart, but we don't pray about it. I am guilty of this. I'll often hear something, check with a friend or mentor, and see if what I sense lines up with Scripture, but I don't ask God more about it.

A few times, though, I have gone back to pray more about something I thought I heard. For example, I have wrestled many times with the idea of starting a side business while I am in ministry with InterVarsity. My mentors and friends have thought this would be fine. It's not against Scripture to start an ethical business. But every time I have had this urge to run with my million-dollar idea or had some green lights to go ahead, I have prayed about it and felt the Spirit tell me no. I know God's voice, and he keeps telling me that he is not yet allowing me to do this. So I have stopped my plans and kept focused on what I hear God calling me to.

Just because something is biblical or your friends think it's a good idea, it may not be what God wants you to do. Ask him, and he will show you what he wants.

Fruit: Will It Help You Become More Like Jesus?

Does what you are hearing make you more loving, joyful, peaceful, patient, kind, good, faithful, gentle and self-controlled—the fruit of the Spirit (Galatians 5:22-23)? Jesus said that a tree is judged by its fruit (Luke 6:43-44), so if what you hear produces different fruit, then it may not be from God. All direct messages from God should strengthen, comfort and encourage (1 Corinthians 14:3), and such messages should convict, not condemn.

Conviction is different from condemnation or shame. Conviction leads us to see that what we are doing is wrong, and we may even feel guilty for what we did. But conviction always includes an invitation on the back end. God may convict us of pride, but he will invite us to a new, humble way. Condemnation, which leads to shame, says that we are bad. Condemnation judges us; conviction judges our actions. Shame-based thoughts, impulses or nudges are not from God.

This is especially important for those of us who are more radical. Sometimes we get an idea to do something for God, but it is not in the right spirit or will not make us more like Jesus. Or we may do something we feel God has asked us to do, but as we reflect on life, or ask our community, we realize we are not becoming more like Jesus. We're more angry, impatient or anxious. It's a clear sign that God is not behind this.

I see this happen more frequently among people who share their faith boldly. They are impatient and do not wait for the proper timing in a seeker's life. Just because we have the good news doesn't mean now is the right time to share it. We often have to build trust by letting relationships develop. If we share the gospel out of impatience, the fruit is not right and God is not in it.

This also goes for anyone who is more timid and shies away from making waves. At times Jesus was bold and confrontational. He got angry at the right things. He also had direct conversations about faith. Some are hiding behind "I don't want to be pushy or unloving" as an excuse to not take a risk or share the faith. That produces zero fruit. By withholding a message from God, these people are not loving others. Jesus was not timid; he was bold. But he was also patient and waited for correct timing. Do not confuse *patience* with *timidity*. Patient witness assumes there is a correct time; timid people shy away even when the time is right.

Community: What Do Other Christians Say About What You Heard?

Jesus reminds us that he is with us when "two or three gather" in his name (Matthew 18:20). And Paul writes that churches "should weigh carefully what is said" in God's name (1 Corinthians 14:29). Our Christian community often hears better for us than we can for ourselves.

We face two major problems when it comes to hearing God in community. One is that some communities abuse this and manipulate others to do things. The other problem is that many Christians make decisions autonomously. They are not submitting anything they hear or do to the community to discern whether it is from God.

The best decisions I make are those I submit to the community God has entrusted me to. When I hear something from God, I quickly share it with my church, my mentors and my closest friends. They have saved me from bad decisions and propelled me with urgency toward the things God was in fact saying to me.

Our church has something called root groups, which are groups of two to four people who gather every other week to discern what God is saying and then act on it. I love my root group. It keeps me accountable to Bible-based people who listen to me share what I think I am hearing from God and discerning with me what to do about it. As long as I keep going to this group, I am protected from getting lost in my own ideas or getting swayed by the enemy.

It makes me sad to watch people receive something they think is from God but keep it from those closest to them because they don't want to hear negative feedback. These people are doing themselves and others a disservice. If you feel that you shouldn't tell others about something you think you heard from God, it probably is not from God.

Response: What Would You Think or Do If Fear Wasn't Involved?

The opposite of faith is not doubt but fear. Scripture reveals that when God shows up, he consistently tells us not to fear (e.g., Isaiah 41:10). In fact, God is love, and perfect love casts out fear (1 John 4:16-18).

Many times our fear blocks our ability to hear what God is saying. I use this question to check whether God is speaking to someone: If you were able to take the fear you feel out of the equation, what would you think or do?

We tend to be full of fear and often justify the decisions we make based on fear. Often, when counseling people who face a difficult decision, the question "What would you do if you had no fear?" unlocks them. Their answer usually is what God is saying. God does not want us to proceed in fear.

One guy I was mentoring had to choose between two jobs. Both jobs were great, and he could have served God in either. But when I asked him, "What would you do if you had no fear?" it became obvious. One job opportunity was gripping him because it had more security and money. As soon as he saw that he was drawn to it because of fear, he opened up more to God and clearly heard his voice.

Results and relationship. The results of a decision you make are not up to you. You may hear and respond correctly, but it still may not turn out the way you want. In fact, you may suffer or be persecuted when you follow Jesus (John 15:20).

What you hear may change, as it did for Abraham (Genesis 22:2, 12). God may tell you one thing at a point in your life, and then tell you a seemingly contradictory thing later. Dallas Willard writes, "We must therefore make it our primary goal not just to hear the voice of God, but to be mature people in a loving relationship with him. Only in this way will we hear him rightly."[2]

GIG Suggestions by Theme

The following GIG (Groups Investigating God) suggestions are organized by particular needs or desires people might have. These were created by a team of InterVarsity staff in San Diego.

Need a Sign from God or Need to Be Amazed by God's Power
John 20:24-31 (Jesus appears to Thomas)
Luke 8:22-25 (Jesus calms the storm)
John 2:1-12 (Jesus turns water into wine)
John 11:17-44 (Jesus raises Lazarus from death)
Mark 6:30-44 (Jesus feeds the 5,000)

Looking for Purpose or Satisfaction
John 4:1-42 (woman at the well)
John 6:25-35 (Jesus is the bread of life)
Luke 5:1-11 (Jesus calls the disciples)
Mark 6:30-44 (Jesus feeds the 5,000)

Struggling with Anxiety
Luke 8:22-25 (Jesus calms the storm)

Wrestling with Guilt or Need God's Forgiveness
Luke 15:11-23 (parable of the prodigal son)
Matthew 18:12-14 (parable of lost sheep)
John 3:1-21 (Nicodemus visits Jesus)
Mark 2:13-17 (Jesus eats with sinners)
Luke 19:1-9 (Jesus visits Zacchaeus's house)

Going Through Painful Circumstances or Need Healing
Matthew 20:29-34 (blind men cry out for mercy)
Mark 1:40-45 (Jesus heals man with leprosy)

Feel Alone, Ostracized or Looking for Belonging
John 4:1-42 (woman at the well)
Mark 5:24-34 (bleeding woman)
Matthew 20:29-34 (blind men cry out for mercy)

Need to Know Everything Before Believing
John 1:35-51 (come and see)
John 9 (religious leaders question the healed blind man)
Mark 5:24-34 (bleeding woman)
John 20:24-31 (Jesus appears to Thomas)
Mark 9:14-29 ("I do believe; help me overcome my unbelief")

Hear the Word but Need Life Transformation
John 9 (Jesus tells blind man to "Go wash")
Luke 8:1-15 (parable of the four soils)

Need to Experience Faith in Action
John 13:1-17 (Jesus washes the disciples' feet)
John 15:1-17 (the vine and the branches)

Need to Take a Risk or to Get Past Big Barriers in the Way of Jesus
Luke 5:17-26 or Mark 2:1-12 (friends help a paralyzed man meet Jesus)
Matthew 14:22-33 (Jesus and Peter walk on water)

Need to Give Up Something for God or Challenged to Sacrifice
Matthew 13:44-46 (parables of hidden treasure and the pearl)
Mark 14:3-9 (woman with perfume)

Need to Hear About Jesus' Death, Resurrection and Love
John 10:1-18 (Jesus the good shepherd)
John 3:1-21 (Nicodemus visits Jesus)

Ready to Commit to Christ
John 10:1-18 (Jesus is the gate for the sheep)
John 20:19-29 (Jesus appears to Thomas)
Luke 23:32-43 (two thieves on cross)
Mark 1:16-20 (fishermen follow Jesus)

Believe in Jesus but Need to Grow
John 16:5-15 (Jesus teaches about the Holy Spirit)
Luke 11:1-13 (Jesus teaches on prayer)

Need Assurance of God's Promises
John 15–16 (Jesus instructs the disciples)

Need to See the Significance of Community
Acts 4:32-35 (the early church)
1 Samuel 18:1-4 (David and Jonathan)

Ready to Lead a GIG
John 4:1-42 (woman at the well)
John 9 (religious leader questioned the healed blind man)

Appendix 3

Conversation Starters

1. What is the most interesting spiritual experience you've ever had?

2. What is your spiritual background?

3. Tell me more about your story—what's your background?

4. What do you think is wrong with the church/Christianity today?

5. Did you grow up in a particular religion? Are you still connected to that faith? (If the answer is no, ask) What changed for you?

6. What's been your experience of Christianity?

7. How would you define success in life? Why do you define it that way?

8. How similar are your personal beliefs about spirituality to your parents'?

9. Tell me about your major. Why did you choose to study that?

10. What kind of things do you do for fun?

11. Tell me about your family. How well do you connect with them?

Appendix 4

Writing Your Lordship/ Transformational Story

What is the area of transformation on which you want to focus?

When you think about this area of life, what was it like before you submitted it to God's control and leading?

How did you come to the decision to submit this area of life to Jesus? What caused you to change your mind (repent) and give God control?

How has God been changing you as you submit this area to him? What fruits of the Spirit are starting to show?

What have you learned about God in the process?

Notes

Chapter 2: Is It Worth It?

[1]Prophecies of the end of exile and the salvation of God's people are spoken of several times in terms of a wedding. Jeremiah 33, especially verse 11, is a great example.

[2]God struck Saul, but Ananias helped him receive Christ and connect to community (Acts 9:1-19).

Chapter 3: Evangelism Is Awkward

[1]Brené Brown, *Daring Greatly: How the Courage to Be Vulnerable Transforms the Way We Live, Love, Parent, and Lead* (New York: Gotham, 2012).

Chapter 4: They're Experience Based

[1]George G. Hunter III, *The Celtic Way of Evangelism: How Christianity Can Reach the West . . . Again* (Nashville: Abingdon, 2000).

[2]These images are from Rick Richardson, *Reimagining Evangelism: Inviting Friends on a Spiritual Journey* (Downers Grove, IL: InterVarsity Press, 2006), pp. 158-59.

[3]More information about Groups Investigating God, including dozens of GIG studies, can be found online at InterVarsity's evangelism website: http://evangelism.intervarsity.org.

[4]Through trial and error, study of culture and my master's program at Wheaton College, I have had some breakthroughs in witnessing to experience-based people. For even more on this see Don Everts and Doug Schaupp, *I Once Was Lost: What Postmodern Skeptics Taught Us About Their Path to Jesus* (Downers Grove, IL: InterVarsity Press, 2008).

Chapter 5: You Are in a Spiritual Battle

[1]Jordan Seng, *Miracle Work: A Down-to-Earth Guide to Supernatural Ministries* (Downers Grove, IL: InterVarsity Press, 2013), p. 15.

[2]Clinton E. Arnold, *Powers of Darkness* (Downers Grove, IL: IVP Academic, 1992), p. 68.

[3]Clinton E. Arnold, *3 Crucial Questions About Spiritual Warfare* (Grand Rapids: Baker, 1997), p. 17.

Chapter 6: Engaging the Spiritual Battle

[1]See Mark Nysewander, *The Fasting Key: How You Can Unlock Doors to Spiritual Blessing* (Ann Arbor, MI: Vine, 2003).

[2]There are many great ministries and books on healing prayer that can teach you how to pray for others, listen for where the Spirit is at work and bring healing and freedom to wounds and strongholds in their lives. Two books I recommend are Neil Anderson, *The Bondage Breaker* (Eugene, OR: Harvest House, 2006); and Rick Richardson, *Experiencing Healing Prayer* (Downers Grove, IL: InterVarsity Press, 2005).

Chapter 7: How to Hear God's Voice in Witness

[1]Dallas Willard, *Hearing God: Developing a Conversational Relationship with God* (Downers Grove, IL: InterVarsity Press, 2012), pp. 20-21, 26.

[2]Ibid., p. 220.

[3]G. Campbell Morgan, *God's Perfect Will* (1901; repr., Eugene, OR: Wipf & Stock, 2004), p. 157.

Chapter 8: God's Role

[1]Craig S. Keener, *The Gospel of John: A Commentary* vol. 2 (Peabody, MA: Hendrickson, 2003), p.1204.

Chapter 9: Your Role

[1]John Teter, *Get the Word Out: How God Shapes and Sends His Witnesses* (Downers Grove, IL: InterVarsity Press, 2003), p. 103.

[2]Neither the demoniac in Mark 5 nor the woman at the well in John 4 were trained before witnessing.

Chapter 10: Don't Miss the Moment

[1]To read more about how to help someone cross the line of faith and accept Jesus, go to my blog www.releasetheape.com.

Chapter 11: How Do I Avoid Being Pushy?

[1]For more on this see J. I. Packer, *Evangelism and the Sovereignty of God* (Downers Grove, IL: InterVarsity Press, 2012).

Chapter 12: How to Turn the Conversation to Jesus
[1]My friend Tyler Allred has a great blog article on Matthew 28 and how we should think about foundation, command and promise. See "Disciple Making: Foundation, Command, Promise," *Tyler Allred* (blog), October 27, 2013, http://tylerallred.net/2013/10/disciplemaking-foundation-command-promise.
[2]See how to write your transformational story in appendix 4.
[3]See how the themes of a person's life are matched with Scripture references in appendix 2.
[4]See Scot McKnight, *A Community Called Atonement* (Nashville: Abingdon, 2007).
[5]See Gustaf Aulén, *Christus Victor: An Historical Study of the Three Main Types of the Idea of Atonement* (New York: Macmillan, 1969).
[6]See Dallas Willard, *The Divine Conspiracy: Rediscovering Our Hidden Life in God* (San Francisco: HarperSanFrancisco, 1998).
[7]Allen M. Wakabayashi, *Kingdom Come: How Jesus Wants to Change the World* (Downers Grove, IL: InterVarsity Press, 2003), p. 37.
[8]Rebecca Manley Pippert, *Out of the Saltshaker and into the World,* 2nd ed. (Downers Grove, IL: InterVarsity Press, 1999), p. 121.

Epilogue
[1]You can read the detailed story on my blog as I take you through how I actually conversed with him and led him to Jesus. Search: "My Neighbor Surrendered His Life to Jesus Today."

Appendix 1
[1]James Choung, *Real Life: A Christianity Worth Living Out* (Downers Grove, IL: InterVarsity Press, 2012), pp. 120-43.
[2]Dallas Willard, *Hearing God: Developing a Conversational Relationship with God* (Downers Grove, IL: InterVarsity Press, 2012), p. 39.

Beyond Awkward Video Campaign

I want to get us talking about our faith as a community!

Make a one-minute video and share it on my blog.

My hope with this video campaign is to get us talking about our faith. I want to give us an opportunity to move beyond the awkward by sharing videos of our stories. Stories where we whiff—where sharing our faith was so awkward. Stories where we saw breakthrough—where Jesus moved powerfully. A number of us have already made videos and are sharing them online. Would you join us? Can we create a community that together is moving beyond awkward in sharing our faith?

Sharing about Jesus is awkward—so why do you do it? Why is it important to you?

What story captures the most awkward time you shared your faith?

What story captures the most powerful time you shared your faith?

On my website I have clear directions about how to make your one-minute video from your phone or computer.

Please join us. It will be so much fun!

Get directions, watch my video, and make your own here:

http://beaucrosetto.com/awkward-videos

 beaucrosetto

 @beaucrosetto

The Forge Missions Training Network exists to help birth and nurture the missional church in America and beyond. Books published by InterVarsity Press that bear the Forge imprint will also serve that purpose.

Beyond Awkward, by Beau Crosetto

Creating a Missional Culture, by JR Woodward

Forge Guides for Missional Conversation (set of five), by Scott Nelson

Incarnate, by Michael Frost

The Missional Quest, by Lance Ford and Brad Brisco

More Than Enchanting, by Jo Saxton

Sentness, by Kim Hammond and Darren Cronshaw

The Story of God, the Story of Us (book and DVD), by Sean Gladding

---

For more information on Forge America, to apply for a Forge residency, or to find or start a Forge hub in your area, visit **www.forgeamerica.com**

For more information about Forge books from InterVarsity Press, including forthcoming releases, visit **www.ivpress.com/forge**